Your
Horoscope
2021

....

Taurus

21 April – 21 May

igloobooks

Published in 2020
by Igloo Books Ltd
Cottage Farm
Sywell
NN6 0BJ
www.igloobooks.com

0820 001
2 4 6 8 10 9 7 5 3 1
ISBN 978-1-83852-324-4

Written by Belinda Campbell and Denise Evans

Cover design by Simon Parker
Edited by Bobby Newlyn-Jones

Printed and manufactured in China

CONTENTS
....

INTRODUCTION

·················

This 15-month guide has been designed and written to give a concise and accessible insight into both the nature of your star sign and the year ahead. Divided into two main sections, the first section of this guide will give you an overview of your character in order to help you understand how you think, perceive the world and interact with others and – perhaps just as importantly – why. You'll soon see that your zodiac sign is not just affected by a few stars in the sky, but by planets, elements, and a whole host of other factors, too.

The second section of this guide is made up of daily forecasts. Use these to increase your awareness of what might appear on your horizon so that you're better equipped to deal with the days ahead. While this should never be used to dictate your life, it can be useful to see how your energies might be affected or influenced, which in turn can help you prepare for what life might throw your way.

By the end of these 15 months, these two sections should have given you a deeper understanding and awareness of yourself and, in turn, the world around you. There are never any definite certainties, but with an open mind you will find guidance for what might be, and learn to take more control of your own destiny.

THE CHARACTER OF THE BULL

....

Steady and grounded, Taurus is a fixed earth sign that the rest of the zodiac can surely rely on. Slow and steady is how this Bull wins the race. Those who have a Taurean in their life should learn to not expect fast results. But boy, when a Taurean delivers, it is likely to be a stunning result. Taurus is known for being one of the most multitalented signs in the zodiac calendar, with a keen eye for the aesthetic. Some of the best artists, makers, writers and creators the world has ever known have been Taureans, such as Salvador Dalí and William Shakespeare.

Lovers of the finer things in life, Taureans may want to surround themselves with beautiful soft furnishings, sparkling jewellery, alluring artwork and other riches. Likewise, Taureans will gorge themselves on equally fine wines and delicious foods. The lure of beautiful things can be constant for Taureans, and whilst this can feel like a cruel fate when money is not free flowing, it can be an added motivation for doggedly pursuing their goals. Perseverance, after all, is what this sign is also best known for. The Taurean love of beauty does not always stop with material things. This springtime sign has a deep connection with Mother Earth. Hiking and working outdoors to enjoy the beauty of the world or finding ways to preserve and protect nature's wonders can be integral to Taureans. The associated colour for Taurus is green and whilst this may be linked to a love of nature, it can also be an indicator of a green-eyed monster that lies within. Possession is a key characteristic of the Bull and whilst this usually relates to material objects, Taureans can sometimes be guilty of treating their loved ones as possessions too.

Jealousy, superficiality and stubbornness are the potential downsides of the talented, nurturing and tenacious Taurean.

THE BULL

Strong and masculine, the Bull inside of Taurus has plenty of charge and direction – there's a reason why everyone aims for the bullseye! The Bull is capable of charging when necessary, similarly Taureans can roll up their sleeves and deliver solid and fast results when life demands it. However, like the Bull, Taureans are more suited to a slower pace of life. Stopping to smell the flowers, taking time to relax in green pastures; this instinct of appreciating Mother Earth should be indulged whenever possible. This sign has an utmost appreciation for the finer things in life, but too often this is translated into material objects and wealth alone. What Taureans value and benefit from most is a long meander through woodlands or reading a good book in the park. Taureans can be accused of being bullish or stubborn, particularly when change is happening that they are uncomfortable with, or if it feels too great or sudden. In ancient Greek mythology, Zeus transformed himself into a white bull and whisked his love Europa to Crete. Zeus's bull has many similarities with Taureans; romantic, tenacious, sometimes possessive and often mystical. Ultimately, the friends and family of a Taurean should feel safe with the Bull by their side, an utmost nurturing and protective symbol that slowly but steadily provides for loved ones.

VENUS

Venus is named after the Roman goddess of love and beauty, so it is no surprise that these very two things govern Taurus. Taureans can happily spend a night at the theatre, ballet or opera, nestled in plush, red velvet seats and revelling in some of the finest displays of beauty and culture with a glass of fine wine. Slaves to their senses, Taureans can take immense pleasure in music, art, dining and, last but not least, physical activities. Encouraged by Venus, tactile Taureans can have a reputation for being sensual lovers. Considered to be some of the most attractive people, guided by their desires and ruled by the planet of love, romance is likely to play a huge role in the life of a Taurean.

ELEMENTS, MODES AND POLARITIES

Each sign is made up of a unique combination of three defining groups: elements, modes and polarities. Each of these defining parts can manifest themselves in good and bad ways and none should be seen as a positive or a negative – including the polarities! Just like a jigsaw puzzle, piecing these groups together can help illuminate why each sign has certain characteristics and help us find a balance.

ELEMENTS

Fire: Dynamic and adventurous, signs with fire in them can be extroverted. Others are naturally drawn to them because of the positive light they give off, as well as their high levels of energy and confidence.

Earth: Signs with the earth element are steady and driven with their ambitions. They make for a solid friend, parent or partner due to their grounded influence and nurturing nature.

Air: The invisible element that influences each of the other elements significantly, air signs will provide much-needed perspective to others with their fair thinking, verbal skills and key ideas.

Water: Warm in the shallows and freezing as ice. This mysterious element is essential to the growth of everything around it, through its emotional depth and empathy.

MODES

Cardinal: Pioneers of the calendar, cardinal signs jump-start each season and are the energetic go-getters.

Fixed: Marking the middle of the calendar, fixed signs firmly denote and value steadiness and reliability.

Mutable: As the seasons end, the mutable signs adapt and give themselves over gladly to the promise of change.

POLARITIES

Positive: Typically extroverted, positive signs take physical action and embrace outside stimulus in their life.

Negative: Usually introverted, negative signs value emotional development and experiencing life from the inside out.

TAURUS IN BRIEF

The table below shows the key attributes of Taureans. Use it for quick reference and to understand more about this fascinating sign.

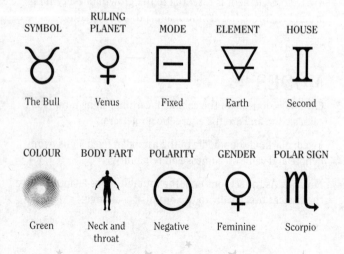

SYMBOL	RULING PLANET	MODE	ELEMENT	HOUSE
The Bull	Venus	Fixed	Earth	Second

COLOUR	BODY PART	POLARITY	GENDER	POLAR SIGN
Green	Neck and throat	Negative	Feminine	Scorpio

ROMANTIC RELATIONSHIPS

· · · · · · · · · · · · · · · · · ·

The slow and steady nature of Taureans means that quick-fire love affairs are unlikely. Instead, they are more likely to find romance blossoming from a friendship, or pursue someone who has been on the outskirts of their life for a while. A sense of security is important to Taureans for their relationships to succeed. An insecure Taurean can turn into a jealous creature that is guilty of suffocating a relationship in a misguided effort to greedily possess a partner. Perhaps the most important lesson for this tempered Bull to learn is how to share a partner's time rather then attempt to dominate it. This is not always an easy task for Taureans, particularly if they come from a small family and are less used to sharing their loved ones. Yet it's an important lesson to practise regularly to keep significant others happy. As with most things, sharing can be easier said than done. Communicating emotions is essential to any successful relationship, and will lead to deeper affection between Taureans and their loved ones.

An ideal partner for a Taurean is one that feeds both the desires and the stomach! Food is essential to the happiness of a Taurean, so the trick to keeping the relationship sweet may be to keep those snack drawers well stocked. A partner who cooks is one that a Taurean will be more inclined to try and keep hold of. Whilst Taureans love to be doted on and thrive on affection from their spouse, they should not be pandered to. A good partner for a Taurean should maintain a level of autonomy and not be tempted to indulge in letting their lover take ownership over them – even if it makes for an easier life! A Taurean's equal should fight to keep their individuality, but also display patience and love. In return, a Taurean will show fierce loyalty and love, for better or for worse.

ARIES: COMPATIBILITY 3/5

The Bull and the Ram may look like two headstrong individuals doomed to clash, but they actually have the potential for a sensual relationship. Whilst their passions for each other are intense, this couple will need to keep a reign on their potential stubbornness and desire to win in order to form a lasting relationship outside of the sheets. The Taurean can be guilty of possessiveness, which the free spirited Arean may struggle with. However, with a joint love of nature and being outdoors, this passionate duo could find their Eden together.

TAURUS: COMPATIBILITY 4/5

This love can be one for the ages. When a Taurean falls for a Taurean, it may be slow and steady as is their usual way or it can be love, and lust, at first sight. These two romantics will shower each other with affection and reciprocate the dedication and loyalty that each deserves. Not one to give up, both Bulls will stand by the other through thick and thin. Should they not see eye to eye, these two are capable of fighting with terrifying passion but will hopefully find that making up is always more fun.

GEMINI: COMPATIBILITY 2/5

Three may prove to be a crowd. The duality of a Geminian, characterised in their Twin symbol, can make a Taurean feel uneasy in starting a romantic relationship with this sign. The Earth sign of Taurus mixed with airy Gemini may not be an easy joining, but if Taurus can budge on their fixed ways then love could grow happily here. Gemini's good communication skills will mean that they should hopefully understand quickly the needs of a Taurus and provide the love and security that Taureans crave in a partner. Communication, trust and flexibility should be this couple's mantra.

CANCER: COMPATIBILITY 5/5

Placed two positions apart on the zodiac calendar, a Cancerian and Taurean share a bond that can feel like home. The Cancerian's frequent displays of love are deep and clear, like two names carved into a tree! The intensity of the Taurean's affection, mixed with the Cancerian's head-over-heels approach, can see these two lovers running to the altar and settling down with babies – not always in that order. Here are two signs that will do anything for each other, and will usually prefer their own little party of two.

LEO: COMPATIBILITY 3/5

Leo is ruled by the Sun and Taurus by Venus; this star and planet are never further away than 48 degrees from each other. The love that these two share is solidified in their sometimes-stubborn commitment to one another. The Lion and Bull are both fixed signs and this can be their undoing in a long-term relationship when neither one is willing to compromise. Both the Lion and Bull will shower each other with affection and admiration, and will boost each other's self-esteem and be a positive influence in their careers. This couple should just be careful to not let their egos get in the way.

VIRGO: COMPATIBILITY 3/5

A Taurean and Virgoan can make for a real power couple. The Taurean's dogged approach to fulfilling goals and the Virgoan's practical and busy mind will see this pair securing a successful future together. The Virgoan can appear overly critical and may end up hurting the Bull's feelings unintentionally. Ruled by Mercury, the planet of communication, the Virgoan can be very attuned to the Taurean's needs and will try to fix any problems within the relationship. These two earth signs will likely share many things in common and can form lifelong companionships, even if a whirlwind romance isn't in the stars.

LIBRA: COMPATIBILITY 4/5

Both ruled by the planet Venus, the love that a Taurean
and Libran share can be a thing of beauty. Their shared
appreciation of culture and aesthetics will have romance
blooming quickly. Wedding bells will ring in both the Taurean
and Libran's ears, and planning for the big day will begin
sooner rather than later. The Libran's airy indecisiveness
can be a point of contention for the grounded Taurean, and
these two won't be without their disagreements. However, the
Libran's diplomacy will help to resolve issues and have them
striving for harmony once more.

SCORPIO: COMPATIBILITY 5/5

Scorpio and Taurus are each other's opposites on the zodiac
calendar, so therefore cosmically share a special relationship
both in their differences and similarities. The element of
Taurus is earth and Scorpio's is water, which usually will
mean that both partners will provide something that the other
desperately needs. Love and passion are both driving forces for
these two. Scorpio has the reputation for being the sexiest of
signs and Taurus the most beautiful, so a physical relationship
should be strong here. Whilst this couple will no doubt enjoy
each other's bodies immensely, their tendencies towards
possession and jealousy will need to be kept in check.

SAGITTARIUS: COMPATIBILITY 2/5

A Sagittarian is ruled by the planet Jupiter, which is associated with luck – something that a Taurean doesn't always believe in. Whilst the Sagittarian values new experiences, the Taurean prefers familiar, safer comforts. The biggest struggle that this fire and earth couple may have is the Sagittarian's need for freedom, and the Taurean's tendency towards possessiveness with a partner. A claustrophobic atmosphere should be avoided, and freedom actively given in this relationship. They must learn from one another; both by admiring the faster gallop of the Centaur, and equally by appreciating the steady plod of the Bull.

CAPRICORN: COMPATIBILITY 3/5

A Capricornian and Taurean in love are loyal and true to each other. These two earth signs value hard work, and are driven by their need to enjoy the fruits of their labours. The home that these two could build together will likely be full of beautiful and expensive objects, with a couple of prized cars jewelling the garage. Whilst both will have dreams of marriage, the Capricornian is the more traditional one and will probably approach the subject first. The Taurean should try to inject joy and fun into the relationship to teach the Capricornian how to enjoy the lighter side of life.

AQUARIUS: COMPATIBILITY 1/5

A Taurean and Aquarian aren't an obvious match on paper, and it's unlikely they will be paired on a dating website. The core differences between these two makes a romantic spark unlikely, but should not be ruled out. The Aquarian is partly ruled by the planet Uranus, symbolising rebellion and change – often the Taurean's worst nightmare. For the easy life-seeking Taurean who likes what they know, the travel-lusting Aquarian can be hard to keep up with. These two signs are both fixed and have the potential to make each other stronger if they remain open to change.

PISCES: COMPATIBILITY 3/5

A Taurean and Piscean are capable of having a highly sympathetic and understanding love together. The practical-minded Taurean should encourage the dreamy Piscean to live out fantasies and work hard, for everyone's benefit. In return, the Piscean will shower the Taurean in waves of love and gratitude for all the support and encouragement. However, the Piscean would be wise to not saturate the relationship emotionally and spoil the Taurean. With the Piscean being a water sign, the Taurean can feel the nourishing effects this sign has on its earth element, and the life that these two can grow together is one well worth living.

FAMILY AND FRIENDS

. . . .

Just as Taureans are dedicated to sticking to their goals, the same steadfast dedication is given to maintaining relationships with friends and family. Taureans want to see loved ones succeed, and will try to offer unfailing support mentally, physically and financially if they can. Positioned under the second house in the zodiac calendar, Taurus has a strong influence with possessions and money. Taureans are not ones to spend all their hard-earned wealth on just themselves, instead they are likely to want to share their fortunes with loved ones. From picking up a cheque for dinner to paying for extracurricular activities for their children, Taureans are generous with their love, time and money.

A Taurean home will clearly display signs of success, wealth and a love for beautiful and opulent design. From decorative throws and pillows, to the artwork hanging on the walls (that may or may not be a Taurean original), to the grand piano taking centre stage, the Taurean home will likely be a stunning display of the beauty in life. Beauty-loving Librans and homemaking Cancerians will value the stylish home that Taureans are capable of building, and can provide some of the most appreciative and kindred of friendships or relatives.

A key characteristic of Taureans is their focus on possession, which can lead them to become workaholics in their desire to be the affluent provider for their family. When it comes to family, it's important for Taureans to remember that the people for whom they are providing are more important than what they are providing. Despite their weakness toward possession, what Taureans are more reliably known for is their unmoving loyalty and stability, both key attributes for building a happy family home. If a Taurean befriends or is related to another Taurean, their relationship will have the strong bones for forming some of the most reliable and steady relationships that the zodiac calendar knows.

Be careful of upsetting Taureans because they can hold a grudge for years and years. They would do well to learn to forgive any friends and family they feel have done them an injustice, if they want to keep that person in their life. Taureans should ask themselves this question: is it more important to hold on to this grudge or to hold on to this relationship? Taureans choose their friendships wisely and will usually be unwilling to let go of their investment in it, even if the friendship has soured or become too toxic to remain close. Taureans should learn to live and let live, and move forwards from any disagreements that they have with their family and friends. If a Taurean chooses to keep a friendship after a falling out, it should be based on forgiveness with an unclouded look towards a happier, shared future.

MONEY AND CAREERS

. . . .

Being a particular star sign will not dictate certain types of career, but it can help identify potential areas for thriving in. Conversely, to succeed in the workplace, it is just as important to understand strengths and weaknesses to achieve career and financial goals.

The mode of Taurus is fixed, rather than cardinal or mutable, which in career terms can mean that once Taureans decide what their career path is, they will stubbornly stick with it until they achieve their goal ambitions. Which career path to take may not always be clear, particularly as they are known for being multitalented. Whilst a career choice may be undecided, belonging to the second house in the zodiac calendar representing wealth will mean that dreams of money and fortune will no doubt be a driving force for all Taureans. A career in finance, such as investment banking, could be a satisfying job, as they will enjoy watching their investments grow over time. High-risk decisions won't be appealing to Taureans. Rather, a steadfast investment is something that will likely attract them to parting with their hard-earned money.

Whilst Taureans may be naturally good at a job in finance, the more negative characteristics associated with this sign, such as greed and being overly materialistic, may mean that this avenue is best avoided to help keep these traits at bay. A more grounded career, influenced by this sign's earth element, may be complementary to a happy work life. The gradual and sustainable process of growing plants or vegetables lends itself to the slow-paced Taurean, so perhaps a career in horticulture would be well suited. Taureans' appreciation of beauty may lead to work in conservation, appealing to their nurturing side and their love of Mother Earth. Whether it is through full-time work or a leisurely activity, being in nature will have a positive and calming effect, and offer balance and perspective.

Ruled by Venus, the planet of beauty, the sign of Taurus has great potential with pursuing a career in the arts. Some of the best-known artists, including Salvador Dalí and William Shakespeare, are Taureans. Taureans strongly value security, and might struggle with the uncertainty of success, financial or otherwise, that a life in the arts can offer. This dislike for unsteady work and working for no immediate money are things that arty Taureans will need to overcome. However, their determination to hone their craft by stubbornly working towards their goals day by day can mean the bright lights of fame and success will be the ultimate pay-off. Taureans are known for not just appreciating beauty but also for being beautiful themselves, so perhaps a career in acting or fashion, like Taurean supermodel Gigi Hadid, may prove fulfilling.

As with family, colleagues cannot be chosen. Therefore, it can be advantageous to use star signs to learn about their key characteristics and discover the best ways of working together. As co-workers, Leonians can have a positive influence on Taureans by encouraging them to make bolder choices. However, Taureans may find Leonians difficult bosses, as neither the Bull nor the Lion is likely to admit defeat graciously. Taureans are multitalented in the workplace, and share many skills with other signs; from their problem-solving initiative that links them with practical Virgoans, to the resolute ambition they share with desirous Scorpians. These appealing attributes, together with their calm and patient nature, make Taureans liked and valued by their colleagues.

HEALTH AND WELLBEING

· · · · · · · · · · · · · · · · ·

Being a lover of the finest food and drink, Taureans can sometimes struggle with keeping their weight down. Not ones to deny themselves the luxury of eating out at fine restaurants, those calories can add up as high as their bill. And what's dinner without dessert? By making more meals from scratch at home, Taureans will be more aware of the ingredients going into their favourite foods. Taureans are known for their pre-planning and organisation skills. By utilising these positive traits in the kitchen, Taureans can prepare healthy meals ahead of time, and ensure that they are eating a more balanced diet.

Taurus rules the throat and neck and, like the Bull, it is often a Taurean's strongest area. Perhaps that is why this sign is known for being home to some of the most famous singers of all time, from James Brown to Ella Fitzgerald and Adele. Even if a Taurean does not enjoy singing, it may be beneficial to take extra care of this area by always wearing a scarf in the colder months, and avoiding drinking too much alcohol that could aggravate the throat.

Bulls are strong with a stocky build, and Taureans often find success in weightlifting or gymnastics. However, Earth is the element that guides Taurus and so physical exercise is likely to be enjoyed more so in Mother Nature than it is in the confines of a man-made gym. Walking is a wonderful form of regular and gentle exercise that Taureans can enjoy at an adjustable speed that is comfortable for them. Not only will walking or running outdoors help with maintaining a level of physical health, it will also make sure that they stay connected to nature where they feel their calmest.

Maintaining a healthy mind is just as important as listening to what the body needs. Taureans can be stubborn and unforgiving of people that they feel have wronged them. If fixated on, this negativity can be extremely harmful for Taureans and may even manifest itself in physical pain, such as a tight neck and shoulders. By practising forgiveness and letting go of negative emotions, Taureans should find that they are much happier and healthier, and are able to refocus on what brings them joy. Exercise that centres on bringing balance to the mind as well as the body, such as yoga or t'ai chi, will help calm the aggravated Bull. Jealousy can also be another internal sore sport for any Taurean. Whilst it is a normal emotion experienced by most, Taureans can feel its sting too often in their relationships, and it may become a real cause of pain if left to fester. By questioning why these feelings of jealousy arise, Taureans can then work towards nipping those negative emotions in the bud.

Taurus

....

DAILY FORECASTS
for 2020

OCTOBER

. . . .

Thursday 1st

A Full Moon in your dreaming sector will show where you hide and retreat and what dreams are possible or just illusions. Take care, as the tendency will be to self-medicate with something that will make you switch off. Better to use alone time to heal and not to isolate yourself. The evening may be best used for a hot bubble bath and a good book.

Friday 2nd

Venus moves into your creative sector and you could now be redecorating your home or revamping your style. Young children will play a part for the next couple of weeks and will teach you how to have fun and laughter. Venus also wants you to learn about self-care. It's a time to look after your mental and emotional wellbeing.

Saturday 3rd

The Moon is making a lovely connection from your sign to Venus. You will feel pleasantly indulgent without going overboard. You may want to have a pamper session at a spa or fill your mind, body and soul with nourishing and beautiful things. They don't have to be big or cost a lot; let yourself do something simple and enjoyable that you don't often get to do. You deserve it.

Sunday 4th

Anything could happen as the Moon passes Uranus in your sign and sits opposite Mercury. You could say something shocking or even hurtful, so be careful with words today and remember to think before you speak. You could use this influence to be innovative and blaze a trail. Just be aware that words can be highly impactful, so choose the impact you want to make carefully.

Monday 5th

Pluto goes direct today, so that means that now all of the planets moving slowly in your travel sector are on-board for more forwards motion. It has been a long time of blocks and frustrations for you, but finally you will see the road you are about to travel. Be willing to see this symbolically and you'll travel further.

Tuesday 6th

Money and possessions will be on your mind, and that will be no surprise to you. You may be in two minds about spending, so get out of your own head and ask someone's advice. You should be feeling positive and upbeat, but be undecided between two choices. Talk it all through with someone who you trust and the decisions should be made easier.

Wednesday 7th

Another day where you should be cautious with words. There is an old saying that asks that before you speak, consider if it is true, kind and necessary. If you remember this then you cannot go wrong and will be less likely to say something shocking. Ask yourself this the next time you go to say something and try and use it as a mantra throughout the day.

Thursday 8th

The Moon moves into the area of your chart that deals with short journeys and communication. This could be a day when you have a lot of little jobs to do or a lot of visits to make. Family is also highlighted here, so small get-togethers are likely. If nothing else, checking in with your nearest and dearest might be a good idea today.

Friday 9th

The two rulers of your opposite sign are not in a good connection today. Pluto in your travel sector is telling Mars in your dream sector that something has to change. Mars does not like this and will stand his ground. Who will win? What needs to change? You're likely to feel conflicted today; take while to consider everything before you make any lasting changes.

Saturday 10th

Venus glosses over any radical behaviour you may have displayed recently. As your ruler, she can mother and nurture you or entice you to be very self-indulgent. Here, she gives you motherly advice and teaches you to laugh at your outspokenness, whilst reminding you not to do it again. There may be vital lessons to learn, here.

Sunday 11th

The Moon in your family sector makes you want to feel like number one today but it is also making uneasy connections to Uranus and Mercury, and your need to be outrageous surfaces once again. Self-control would be useful today, as would keeping a clear head and not doing anything too spontaneous. Be warned, repeated rash behaviour will not end well for you.

Monday 12th

Today you will be thinking about the recent past and wondering what on earth made you say or do something that did not put you in good light. You do not like to be thought of badly, so you must think of a way to put things right now. Reflecting on your own actions and seeing if you need to make a change might also be a right step forward.

Tuesday 13th

Aggressive actions will be exposed today. These could be yours or another's directly affecting you. This could even just be thoughts in your head. Watch your blood pressure and other health issues as you are not doing yourself any favours. Take a deep breath and employ any healthy coping mechanisms you may have.

Wednesday 14th

Now you have Mercury retrograde in your sector of relationships, which means your recent reckless words and behaviour are not going to be forgiven just yet. Your negative mood will continue for a couple of weeks and you will be a raging bull. Again, watch your health.

Thursday 15th

Advice for the next couple of days is to concern yourself with your day-to-day duties, as it could help balance out your irritable mood. It is best not to expect too much from others, so keep your head down and just get on with the jobs you need to. This mood will pass.

Friday 16th

A New Moon in your health and routine sector is urging you to find balance between work and play. Take a good look at which health routines you could change or make better, and what daily routines are just not necessary or are draining your resources. Find some space each day to make sure that you do something for yourself.

Saturday 17th

Remember that Mercury retrograde in your relationship sector? Today the Moon passes over it and also sits opposite Uranus, who likes to upset the status quo. Today is not a good one for romance, so stay in and wash your hair. If you live with a partner, tensions may run high. Just be mindful of your words and actions.

Sunday 18th

Today you will have a lesson about boundaries. You will learn where you end and another person begins. This will most likely be your partner or the most significant person in your life. Give the other some space and remember that you are two separate people. This may come as a direct result of yesterday's unsettled romantic energy. Ask yourself if there are any lessons to be learned here.

Monday 19th

Venus and Mars are both making connections to Jupiter in your travel sector. Venus is speaking kind words of service and duty, but Mars is making his own problems bigger by not listening to good advice. Try to listen and keep a level head. Dreams and goals are blocked today, but they are just dreams and nothing tangible yet.

Tuesday 20th

Be careful, as anything could happen. The shock factor is still with you, so see if you can turn that around and make it into a nice surprise for someone special. The Moon is asking you to look at how you can be kind to others today.

Wednesday 21st

The Moon moves into your travel sector today and your thoughts return to far-off lands. Venus is having a nice conversation with Uranus, the God of Change, because she wants something from him. What is it you would like? Maybe just ask for it. The results might surprise you.

Thursday 22nd

The Sun enters your relationship sector so the mood could be a little lighter in this area, although it also means the spotlight is not on you. Can you handle that? You want to move forwards in your travel plans again today. Look out for signs of change and progress.

Friday 23rd

Your career is in focus, so is there something you want to speak out about? Can you do this with respect and honesty? Your ruler, Venus, is giving you a helping hand to say what is on your mind without causing any upset. Venus wants to serve you well. Use this opportunity.

Saturday 24th

Venus is helping you out once more. She is talking to Saturn, the teacher, in your travel sector and learning what she can from him about how to plan your future correctly. Listen to what Saturn says as his advice, though sometimes harsh, is always the best. Prepare for the possible arrival of some home truths.

Sunday 25th

Mercury has nothing to say to you. Instead, he wants you to listen with your heart. The Moon enters your social sector and is making nice connections to your feelings about the past and future. Some time spent with friends and social groups can help you hear what your heart has to say.

Monday 26th

Today has the potential to be quite a delightful day. Your emotions can feedback to your mind and be held there without the need for action. You should be able to feel at peace and some welcome surprises could come your way. Give thanks for friendships and support groups today.

Tuesday 27th

Your mood is still light and airy with some positive vibes about your travel plans. You can now see what were always going to be impossible dreams and what are new true possibilities. The lack of action at the moment does not matter; it is all still in the planning stage and in a much better position.

Wednesday 28th

As the Moon drifts into your dreaming sector, Mercury wants you to take another look at the balance between what you think and what you say. Venus enters the beginning of your health and routine sector and is also asking you to check the balance here. Look at your current routine and behaviours and ask yourself if everything you're doing is necessary.

Thursday 29th

You may feel a little irritable and want to move onwards, but have learned a valuable lesson in waiting until the big picture is clearer. Use that tension to do something good for your body. Go for a walk, a run or put energy into something nurturing. Find some healthy distractions to keep your mind and body busy while you wait for time to pass.

Friday 30th

The Moon enters your own sign which, as always, can make you self-indulgent and obnoxious. Enjoy something that will benefit your health now. Take a look at what you have done before to feel good in your body or try some new type of exercise or food. You need to find ways to look after yourself, but they don't always have to be boring.

Saturday 31st

A Full Moon in your sign could mean that you will be a little unpredictable today. The Sun is shining on Uranus in your sign too, so the shock factor could return. Make sure that your behaviour does not upset anyone, particularly your significant other or someone close to you. Tread carefully and me mindful of your words and actions.

NOVEMBER

....

Sunday 1st

Your heart expands a little and emotions get bigger, but there is happiness here. There is a nice connection between the Moon in your sign and Jupiter in another earth sign. You feel positive and optimistic today. The Sun shines on any factors that may disrupt and antagonise you. Make the most of it and see where it can be used to your advantage.

Monday 2nd

The Moon moves into your money sector and makes a nice, easy connection to Saturn who will teach you something about where your money is going. A good day for finances, whether that be saving or spending. You will know your limits today.

Tuesday 3rd

Sex appeal and romantic thoughts are on your side. Your energy and drive to please someone and make harmony in your love life is strong, and you will be fair and tender. You can pursue what you desire, but with compassion. Making even a small gesture could be appreciated as much as a grand gesture.

Wednesday 4th

Mercury resumes a forwards motion today and this helps smooth over any upsets you may have experienced in the retrograde period. You can begin to put things right in your love life and also your daily routines. Health will pick up again and you will feel better about yourself. Look back over anything which has not gone according to plan recently and aim to put things right.

Thursday 5th

The Moon moves into your sector of short trips, siblings and communication. However, it is not in a good position to your ruler Venus, so you will need to put your needs to one side and do a little bit of running around pleasing other people. Today might be a day of putting everyone else before yourself, even if you don't particularly want to.

Friday 6th

Watch your temper. Your mood does not match your energy and you will become agitated and possibly aggressive. Maybe you feel you have done too much for other people and not enough for yourself recently. Keep your cool as this will pass quickly. Avoid doing or saying anything which you might find yourself regretting in a day or two when this passes.

Saturday 7th

Yesterday's mood continues and you will have to curb that instinct to show off, especially in front of your family. Avoid sulking or shouting, as these will not make you look very good when you genuinely want or need attention in the future. You may need to exercise mindfulness and patience. Be a model family member today.

Sunday 8th

Whilst the Sun is in Scorpio, your opposite sign, you will be looking at the shadow side of yourself. This is a golden opportunity to dig for gold deep down in your psyche, but the tendency is to stamp about and demand that you are the centre of attention. That is your shadow. Try not to let it take over.

Monday 9th

Tensions are still high today as Venus, your ruler, opposes her lover, Mars. Venus wants peace and harmony in your daily routine, but Mars wants action. Resist the urge to upset the status quo, Venus knows best in this situation. Act with patience and with kindness.

Tuesday 10th

Today you may have a last-minute chance to say what is on your mind and deep in your heart. Psychology might not really interest you but, if you can find someone willing to talk, you may find out something of deep value concerning how you relate to other people. Today should present chances and opportunities to explore yourself.

Wednesday 11th

Your travel plans come back into your mind and you notice that the yearning is still there. Work or play? Why not both? How can you do this? Can your career be combined with travel or your other interests? Look at the possibilities and a new possibility might present itself.

Thursday 12th

The Moon in your routine and health sector sits next to Venus, and they discuss your desires and how to take care of yourself. Whilst this is happening, Jupiter and Pluto meet in your travel sector. This forebodes a change that dives so deep that life might never be the same again. See how you can influence this for the better.

Friday 13th

Listen carefully and explore all avenues today, as that change in your travel and work sector may be just the thing you have been seeking this year. The Moon passes through your love sector and is helping you scan the bottom of your soul to bring things to the surface.

Saturday 14th

Mars goes direct in your sector of dreams and solitude today, which means that any plans, visions and solitary pursuits will have the green light. You will now see momentum in this area. Things are finally moving forward for you. Choose which directions you want them to go.

Sunday 15th

A New Moon in your love sector suggests that your focus is now on loving, balanced relationships. However, this New Moon is deep, dark and secretive, and can transform anything it touches. Are you ready for a relationship like that? This could be disastrous or healing. Be careful what you wish for at this time.

Monday 16th

Luck and love are at odds, so it is best not to push things as you will probably come away the loser. The Moon is still in your love sector and things could be intense, but not in a good way. Stick to the mundane activities today to err on the safe side and act with caution on anything which isn't strictly routine.

Tuesday 17th

Someone might want to talk about matters which touch them deeply, but you are likely not willing to listen. This could also be the deepest parts of you wanting to surface. Chaos in the head and old behaviour patterns could cause some outrageous actions. Be careful of how you step and try not to let that temper show.

Wednesday 18th

You have the urge to keep pushing on certain issues. Hopefully, these are your own issues that need working out. If they do involve another person then you should learn to be driven but compassionate. You can be motivated today, but emotionally drained by it all. Remember to try and pace yourself.

Thursday 19th

The mood lifts. You will be willing to recognise restrictions and boundaries and will once again be yearning for distant lands. You want to try something new and foreign to you, and you have more respect for other kinds of people. Listen carefully and you may learn something today; an open mind is key.

Friday 20th

The Moon enters your career sector, but it is not a favourable day and you will need to watch what you say and do. Controversial behaviour and speaking without thinking will be the flavour of the day. You want to say and do what is on your mind, but beware. Things which you might usually get away with may not be taken so lightly today.

Saturday 21st

Venus enters your opposite sign of Scorpio which can bring some zest to your love life, and with the Sun entering your sector which deals with sex, death and rebirth, you could be in for a very interesting time. These transits could also show your shadow side.

Sunday 22nd

The Moon in your social sector adds a dream-like quality to your love life. Is it too good to be true? You may now see yourself reflected in another person, and you must take care to recognise borders and know what is you and what is the other. Try to keep your head tightly screwed on and your feet firmly on the ground.

Monday 23rd

Sweet-talking your significant other or anyone who means a lot to you comes easy today. You are still in a floaty, dreamy mood and you will need to see what is real and what is an illusion. If you veer towards illusions then something could dissolve in front of your eyes.

Tuesday 24th

You will be wanting to act on your fantasies. Talking about them with another gives you the urge to make them real. Take heed from the last few days that all that glitters is not gold, and see things and people for what and who they really are. Remember to keep a firm grip on reality and try not to float away.

Wednesday 25th

Are you projecting your ideals onto others? If people start to disappoint you then you probably are. Building castles in the sky is the same as making sandcastles. Very soon they will come crumbling down and leave you wondering why you made the effort. Understand that not everyone thinks like you do.

Thursday 26th

The Moon meets Mars today and you can feel victimised or blocked in your plans. Take some time out today before aggression builds and go and do something physical. Just spending time alone with a good book or TV show might ease the tension and keep you safe.

Friday 27th

There could be some issues in your love life today. Beware of volatile and selfish behaviour. You may experience some nasty surprises if you insist on provoking someone who holds an opposing point of view. Power struggles and control issues can be settled if you see both sides. Try not to restrict yourself to your own perspective.

Saturday 28th

You need the larger group around you today. You want someone to agree with you and have the same philosophies as you. You do not want to stand out in the crowd as being wrong about something. You want to gather an army of support around you. Find solace in a like-minded individual if you can.

Sunday 29th

Today is an easier day than of late. You will know that only a Taurean can best meet their own needs by indulging in a little luxury or having a spending spree. Conversations are pleasant and the day goes quite smoothly. Enjoy this better atmosphere while you can.

Monday 30th

A Full Moon in your money sector will ask you to take a good look at what you have and what you need. You could be in two minds about this and will struggle to see if there is anything that you actually just do not need. Be firm with yourself and be ready to let things go.

DECEMBER

. . . .

Tuesday 1st

Today Mercury enters your house of sex, death and rebirth with an enquiring mind that wants your thoughts about recent issues. Do you want to talk about it? You may feel like sharing your thoughts with someone special. See if you can find someone on your level or who shares your views and throw some ideas around.

Wednesday 2nd

You may be a busy little bull today. You will have lots of little tasks to do and many people to see. Sharing news and gossip with siblings or catching up with messages will be the theme of the day. Nothing spectacular will happen, but things will get done.

Thursday 3rd

Your mood is not in line with your drive today. You could feel a bit stuck in the mud and unable to get things moving. This may only be in your thinking, so today is the perfect day to relax and wallow in your dreams, visions and fantasies. Let your mind and imagination run free ready for a time when you'll have the energies to make things happen.

Friday 4th

You could get a little creative today and have some fun with it. Family surround and encourage you. Remember to act from the heart today and not from the ego, as your underlying mood just wants to be centre of attention. Play nicely and you'll reap the benefits.

Saturday 5th

If you act with good intentions today and see a job to its conclusion, you could expect a reward. Be careful though, because Uranus in your sign can bring surprises or nasty shocks. It all depends on the energy you are putting out there to begin with. The more you invest, the more you'll receive, just make sure you making the right sort of investment.

Sunday 6th

You may want to assess the past and future with regards to where you have come from and where you would like to go. It is okay to dream about future plans, but do remember how things worked out for you in the past and do not repeat mistakes.

Monday 7th

Be good to yourself today as the Moon in your leisure sector may leave you feeling exhausted. Do only what is necessary and leave extras alone for today. Pencil in some fun time that will uplift you and make you feel buoyant and joyful. Look after yourself and focus on things which will be of benefit to you.

Tuesday 8th

Positive and easy-going vibes will be sent towards your travel sector. Have you managed to find a way of combining work with your desire to explore? Use today to look again at this possibility. Your heart pulls you towards something new and you should now see what you are able to do about it.

Wednesday 9th

Trying to find a balance between head and heart gets easier today, although you will still need to see what is illusion and what is reality. What is keeping you from seeing the truth? Take off the rose-coloured spectacles and see for yourself. Remember to be pragmatic and realistic in your approach rather than romantic or idealistic.

Thursday 10th

Do things that you can control, today. Your ruler, Venus, is talking to Pluto, who likes to use his power to change and control. He is also the ruler of Scorpio, your opposite sign, so this could mean that these issues are around your partner. There's nothing wrong with playing it safe for a change.

Friday 11th

Relationships from the past might come back, so prepare for these as they could bring up some issues that you have long forgotten about. They may also reveal the reasons why you behave as you do in significant relationships. Is this something that still serves you? Address what needs to be addressed and learn to move on from things which don't.

Saturday 12th

The Moon meets Venus in Scorpio today, so there could be more issues surrounding past or current partners. Mars is also making you dream of past love and comparing this to what you have or what you want now. Some things are best left in the past, however. Time to move on now.

Sunday 13th

You are still thinking about partners past and present. You may also be thinking about finances that you have lost. On the other hand, you may be thinking about investing and sharing something valuable with your partner or someone else important to you. It's usually better to embrace the future than to mourn for the past. Seek some wise advice first.

Monday 14th

A New Moon in your sex, death and rebirth sector sits right on top of chatty Mercury so you can talk about what has been on your mind recently. You have a chance to talk about money too. This comes easily to you but maybe not to others, so be tactful.

Tuesday 15th

Venus moves on and now sits in your sex, death and rebirth sector. She will help you transform outdated patterns and habits and make something shiny and new from them. Love can go up a level and also down to some deep places that you never knew existed. Try to keep an open mind and be ready to grow.

Wednesday 16th

Who is in control now? Has someone or something captured you so tightly that you have surrendered to their grip? This could be an idea, a plan or a person with whom you are enamoured now. Try to stay grounded and dig those hooves in. You do not want to lose your grip on reality.

Thursday 17th

Big things are happening for you, and you are being swept
away with the current. First your mood turns to expansion
and you have great joy and big plans, but then you seem to
be knocked back into moodiness and feel limited. This is the
Moon talking. Learn what there is to be learned and try to keep
a balanced outlook.

Friday 18th

Your mind may feel unsettled and you'll likely feel that you
just cannot get a grip on it today, and that is because Mercury
is absent without leave in your sex, death and rebirth sector.
Try to have a quiet day today and switch off with some fantasy
reading or viewing. Do not overtax your brain today.

Saturday 19th

There could be some tension today as Jupiter is on the last
degree of your travel sector. It feels like you are waiting for a
green light or like something is holding you back. Meanwhile,
the Moon drifts into your social sector so this would be a good
time to go out with friends and distract your mind from your
frustrations.

Sunday 20th

The tension gets bigger today and almost tears you apart. You
have a lot of nervous energy and do not know how to use it.
Jupiter and Saturn are sitting together at the beginning of
your career sector and having a board meeting. This will be the
decider for your future. As difficult as it can be for you, try to
rest patiently today and trust that what will be will be.

Monday 21st

It's the shortest day of the year and here you are waiting for results from Jupiter and Saturn. The tension is electrified by the Sun and Mercury now entering your travel sector. This is looking good, so stay real and leave the celebrations until later. It may feel as if you're not steering your own car today; try to sit back and let the journey happen, for now.

Tuesday 22nd

How much longer can you hold this tension? The Moon now passes into your dreams sector and allows you to indulge in some fantasy. What are your wildest dreams? Do you want to keep them to yourself for a little longer or share the love? Allow your mind to drift and let it be your escape today.

Wednesday 23rd

Today it might feel like everything is going against you. Mars the warrior in your dream sector is squaring off with Pluto the transformer in your travel sector. These are co-rulers of Scorpio, your opposite sign, so you could look at your shadow and see where you are sabotaging yourself.

Thursday 24th

The Moon enters your sign on Christmas Eve and you will tend to overdo it on all the seasonal goodies. It is the holidays and so you deserve it, but do not turn it into a selfish moment and end up as the fatted calf for tomorrow's dinner. Try to exercise some moderation today.

Friday 25th

Merry Christmas! If you did not go to excess yesterday, then today you will be bouncing all over the place like a small child. If you did, then that is another story and you may find yourself lurching around in a bit of a mood. Slow down, it's Christmas!

Saturday 26th

It is the morning after, and you just want to sit and watch some old movies. Do that, because it is just the thing to recover from what has been a year of nail-biting tension and pent-up frustrations. Use it as a relaxed bonding time with family or friends, maybe see if you can use it to have a bit of a laugh as you unwind.

Sunday 27th

Today you will be looking with satisfaction at your Christmas gifts. You will be checking your bank balance and making a note to deal with it in the new year. For now, you are happy to enjoy the remainder of the holiday season with family and friends. Let yourself do this without feeling guilty.

Monday 28th

Already, you are considering what the new year will bring and making resolutions. You might surprise yourself with what you come up with. You could be quite selfish today and not in the mood for love, but do not trouble your loved ones as this mood will pass soon. Just try not to dampen the mood of anyone else.

Tuesday 29th

The last Full Moon of the year lands in your sector of short trips and messages late in the day. Is there anyone you need to catch up with before the festive season ends? This Moon will highlight the need for you to always check in with your loved ones and keep the family bonds of love. Start tying up the year as you mean to go on.

Wednesday 30th

The Moon opposite Mercury today means that your head and heart will have a small battle and you will be torn between family and career. You may find yourself looking at where your home is and the home you have created for yourself. This can be a floaty day for you.

Thursday 31st

A mixed end to the year. The Moon is at home and wants you to be, too. You do not have the energy to argue with anyone or to be the one in charge. Enjoy the last day of 2020 and have a good time reminiscing about what the year has taught you without overexerting yourself.

Taurus

....

DAILY FORECASTS
for 2021

JANUARY

· · · · · · · · · · · · · · · · ·

Friday 1st

Happy New Year and welcome to 2021. The year begins with the Moon in your family sector. Here you are the golden child and can be treated with awe. Spending time with your loved ones will highlight this. Enjoy the closeness of family and feel the love at this festive season.

Saturday 2nd

Have you run out of steam? Are there dreams of yours that have been pushed to one side over the holidays? Time to reclaim your dreams and visions and own them for yourself. You need to act if you wish to manifest them. Mars in your dreams sector will help.

Sunday 3rd

Don't be too hard on yourself today. You are allowed to be creative and playful. It may be tempting to tidy up your inbox and file away that stash of letters, but use today to express yourself in some way. You might surprise yourself and others by letting yourself go.

Monday 4th

It may be a case of your own needs versus those of others today. If you stay on one side, your own side, you may be able to see through fakers and illusionists. On the other hand, if you choose to join groups you will get sucked into an unattainable reality. Be cautious.

Tuesday 5th

If you can keep your mind on the daily grind, then today will tick along nicely. You may experience power issues in the area of travel and higher education. This may feel like someone wants to gag you or dispute an opinion you hold. Watch out for the way this triggers your inner child.

Wednesday 6th

It is imperative that you complete a project that you have spent a lot of energy on. If this is more like a wish or dream, then try to put the finishing touches on any research you have done. Your vision board should be ready for the manifesting stages soon.

Thursday 7th

Mars moves into your sign today. You will feel more assertive and energetic now. This could also be a sexy time as Mars has entered the home of his celestial lover, Venus. It will be easy for you to get what you desire now, so be careful what you wish for.

Friday 8th

As the Moon shifts into your relationship sector, you should be focusing on someone special in your life. If you are single, now is the time that your shadow can reveal itself by projecting your deep moods onto another. Play your cards right and today could be another sensual day.

Saturday 9th

Venus shifts into your travel sector as Mercury flies into your career sector. Note your attraction to all things exotic now and keep your ears open in the workplace. A tasty foreign meal with a partner or simply for yourself will be just the right thing today. Enjoy it.

Sunday 10th

Listen to your elders today. A relative or co-worker who you admire has information or teachings for you to learn from. Authority figures will be helpful resources today. You are willing to listen to deep and meaningful conversations which may benefit you in the long run. Ignore the superficial and dig deep.

Monday 11th

Mercury meets up with Jupiter who asks for truth, justice and expansion. This could be gossip that reaches you and is greatly exaggerated. On the plus side, this could be a change in fortune in the way you communicate at work. This is an ideal time to ask for a raise.

Tuesday 12th

Watch what you say today. Mercury is squaring off to Uranus who likes to shock. This could be a radical change of thinking or an off the cuff remark that will hurt. You may have a 'eureka!' moment or you could start a revolution. Perhaps you should think just a little more before you speak.

Wednesday 13th

The first New Moon of the year occurs in your travel sector. This is an ideal time to set intentions and goals for the coming year. Has higher education attracted you? Could you combine a new learning course with some exotic locations? You may be in two minds about taking a new direction.

Thursday 14th

You will see a battle of egos and wills today. There will be much to learn if you can remain an outsider and watch this play out. Lies can be exposed or someone, maybe you, will be inflating their ego and throwing their weight around. Best not to get involved.

Friday 15th

Keep your head down and get the job done today. There is tension lingering from yesterday and everyone needs to go lick their wounds. Some people may still be up on their soapboxes and preaching their truth. Step down and put your mind into your work for now.

Saturday 16th

Find your tribe today and connect with like-minded people. You are not always a sociable creature but do your best and let that inner bull go for a swim. Being part of a herd will do you good now. There is fun to be had in numbers if you wish.

Sunday 17th

One day of socialising may just have been all you could take. Uranus in your sign is irritated by Jupiter in your career sector. There may be a clash of personalities. Someone larger than life could stir up some trouble and rock the boat. Fasten your life jacket.

Monday 18th

Today it might feel like you are the only one on this planet making any sense. In fact, what is happening is that your dream sector, which is fiery and proactive, is having a visit from the Moon. You will be actively playing your 'get out of jail free' card.

Tuesday 19th

Your career sector will get a boost now as the Sun heats things up. This can result in more responsibility or credit given for a job well done. You can truly shine now and be a good leader for others. Communication is easy today to say what you want.

Wednesday 20th

Aggression can be a problem today. The two planets which like disruption and action are sitting together in your own sign, which might make you the stereotypical raging bull. The Moon also enters your sign, making you more emotional than usual. Use that pent-up energy wisely and find a physical outlet such as going to the gym.

Thursday 21st

This is also unlikely to be a good day for you. There is too much tension for you to cope with and you are at risk of exploding. You may feel blocked and restricted at every turn. Frustration is an understatement. Physical exercise is the only way to get you to focus.

Friday 22nd

You should be getting back in control. Outside events calm down and you'll feel more settled. There can be a lot of mind chatter today and head versus heart battles can surface. This is just a passing phase, so practise controlled breathing and do not act out. You can do this.

Saturday 23rd

At last, the weekend is here, and you need to let off some steam. Visiting friends or family and having the space for a safe rant will benefit you. Venus and Neptune are connecting well, meaning that you can switch off if you wish. Good food is on the menu.

Sunday 24th

Father figures, teachers, bosses or people you admire are in focus today. Take heed of any good advice from elders. You feel more forward thinking and may start planning future home improvements or money-making schemes. Share your ideas with friends and those you trust to give honest feedback.

Monday 25th

Your sense of self is challenged today. How will you react? It may be something like being called on to justify your actions at work. This makes you feel small and hits a childhood wound inside you. This evening would be best spent with comfort foods and your favourite TV shows.

Tuesday 26th

Humiliation is something that you are unable to deal with. Today you are advised to lie low and self-soothe. There is nothing a Taurus likes best than spending money, so maybe a little retail therapy would be good for you. Treat yourself to some tasty foods for a nice evening in.

Wednesday 27th

Your ruler, Venus, has an upset from the Moon. Do not feel guilty about being self-indulgent yesterday. There can be power struggles in the workplace again and will most likely involve women. Keep up with the home comforts and self-nurturing until this tension passes you by.

Thursday 28th

Today there is a Full Moon in your family sector. Unfortunately, this makes several bad connections to other planets and will not be an easy illumination. You could be throwing your weight around with your family or acting like a stroppy teenager. Tantrums are not the way to feel better.

Friday 29th

The Sun and Jupiter sit together in your career sector. This is a lucky combination for you, you will be seen for what you are worth and praise may come your way. This influence can also mean that egoists and manipulators will be exposed for what they are.

Saturday 30th

Today you have a warning. Mercury will go retrograde tomorrow, so use today to back up your devices and check all travel plans. Expect communication problems and misunderstandings in the next three weeks and avoid signing contracts if you can. Practise the pause before responding in any uneasy situations.

Sunday 31st

Mercury retrograde begins. This will happen in your career and responsibility sector. The recent tension may have been the fore-runner of this, so you may already have a taste of what will come. Today you can be creative but be precise and thorough with all communications. Check every tiny detail today.

FEBRUARY

. . . .

Monday 1st

You may see ego battles today. Someone in the workplace may try to humiliate and bring you down. Venus, your ruler, moves into your career sector today meaning that for the next few weeks you have a planetary ally at work. She will help you maintain harmony and dignity.

Tuesday 2nd

Attending to the daily grind will occupy your mind today. Health could be an issue now so use this time for checkups or to schedule appointments. Make sure that you are getting enough time for yourself and finding that work-life balance. You should feel good about yourself today.

Wednesday 3rd

Spend time with a special person, if you can. The Moon favours your intimate relationships. However, Mars and Venus will square off in the evening so be careful not to get bitten by Mercury retrograde. Get deep and sexy but be mindful of boundaries and do not push too far.

Thursday 4th

Expect the unexpected and keep tight control on your temper today. The Moon sits opposite Mars and Uranus in your sign and these two together can be explosive. You may be touchy and sensitive. If something does blow up, it can be larger than you anticipate, so be careful.

Friday 5th

Intensity crackles in the air around you. You could appear as quite controlling of other people but there is a way around this. Use this tension to pull out a lesson you can learn or teach another. This energy will ease by evening and your spirits lift nicely.

Saturday 6th

Venus and Saturn are having a chat in your career sector. This could be someone getting what they deserve at work. Female associates could sweet-talk their way into positions of power. Social networking can be where Venus has her say today. High climbers will lead the way.

Sunday 7th

This weekend has been focused on work and your connections in organisations. You might look back at the past and give thanks to people who have influenced you in your career. There may be someone who has been rattled by another's rising; prepare for some outbursts of jealous rivalry.

Monday 8th

Today you must keep your ears open and be alert to any information you receive. Stay alert as you may well benefit from a casual piece of gossip or an off-the-cuff remark. Tune in to atmospheres and subtle undertones and you may discover some home truths about someone.

Tuesday 9th

Try not to be manipulated today. Also, avoid being the one doing the manipulating. If you must try to coerce someone into agreeing with you, use the gentle art of persuasion. Soft talk and compliments go further than the bullish attitude you can sometimes adopt. Easy does it, remember.

Wednesday 10th

The Moon passes many planets today and all of them in your career sector. This can make you feel uncertain as to what is going on. You are the proverbial dog chasing his tail. Sit back, take a deep breath and let it pass. This is only for today.

Thursday 11th

You will need to be extra careful now as your energy and emotions are not at ease. You will feel irritated and eager to say something that you really shouldn't. Keep it to yourself. A New Moon in your work sector allows you to set new goals and intentions.

Friday 12th

Playing the part of the revolutionary suits you. If there is something wrong that needs rectifying, you are not slow to point it out. You can be a leader when you want to, and you wallow in the credit. Try to be the peacemaker instead; share some time with friends.

Saturday 13th

A dreamy Moon in your social sector has you on a mission this weekend. The romantic idealist surfaces in you and you may lead a party on a day out to somewhere beautiful. Keeping the peace is difficult today with Venus meeting up with Mercury in retrograde. Do what you can.

Sunday 14th

Finish the weekend with another day of eating and drinking well with friends. It will be action stations again tomorrow. Conversations may be free of Mercury's influence today as he sits with lucky Jupiter, who just loves to have a good time. Enjoy your time of precious indulgence with your acquaintances.

Monday 15th

The Moon enters your dreams and visions sector. You are more inclined to make commitments to your future now. This is a good time to make a vision board, bullet points or mental maps of where you want to go in your life. Listening to dream messages will help you.

Tuesday 16th

You have a good idea of how you can once more use skills learned in the past. These can propel you into your dream future. There may be an element of control going on today which will concern higher education and travel. You may resist learning something new.

Wednesday 17th

As the Moon moves into your own sign you will feel more determined. This energy helps to fix your plans in your head. You may resent the self-discipline it takes and have a mini-tantrum, but ultimately you see the reasoning behind it. You must work for what you want.

Thursday 18th

The Sun now enters your social sector and will bring you more empathy and connection with groups and organisations. There is a very good chance that you will over-spend or over-eat today. Be careful that you are not too stubborn and watch that temper, especially with women.

Friday 19th

A battle of the sexes can occur today as Venus and Mars, the celestial lovers are not in a good connection. You will most likely notice this in the workplace. You have Mars in your sign, so you are likely to be the aggressor in this situation. Your ruler Venus will not thank you.

Saturday 20th

Communication is necessary to avoid misunderstandings now. Remember that Mercury is still retrograde. You have luck on your side with a Jupiter connection, but the hard work is down to you. You may have to eat humble pie today. Own any misgivings on your part and play nicely.

Sunday 21st

Mercury turns direct today, but you are not out of the woods just yet. Networking and conversations will still need to be guarded. Remember to respond and not react. Listening is just as essential as talking, you may need reflection time before answering someone. Try not to be overly provocative.

Monday 22nd

Is it possible to connect with family today? Your inner child needs nurturing and may yearn for a comfort blanket or two. You may also be the nurturer. If someone needs your support, then do the right thing and give it. Someone somewhere needs a hug today.

Tuesday 23rd

What has broken through your tough exterior? Today's energy is soft, surreal and brings out a side of you that not many see. This will be most evident in your social circle and your siblings' sectors. You may find yourself sending a lot of comforting messages and energy to someone in need.

Wednesday 24th

Today you may get out your soapbox and start rooting for the underdog. You sense an unfairness and simply must do something about it. This afternoon may see you playing the role of the golden child of the family. Express yourself well now and you will be praised.

Thursday 25th

This is a difficult day as the Moon makes several connections to the planets in your career sector. This will pass very quickly but will make you feel on edge. Remember your responsibilities and be firm and fair. Venus swims into your social sector to lighten things up.

Friday 26th

What would you like to do for yourself today? You will feel pulled in different directions as everyone wants a piece of you. It is a family versus friends day today. By evening you will know the right thing to do, which of course is duty first.

Saturday 27th

A Full Moon comes to highlight your daily service sector. It will also show where you have been neglecting your health. Alternatively, you may now be able to express your own needs or see where your hard work had paid off. Check all the small details today.

Sunday 28th

There is beautiful grounding energy for you to use today. This is so good for you as an earth sign. Use this day to get out in nature, eat some tasty food and get in touch with your senses. Dreams and fantasies will pass you by today as you need something tangible now.

MARCH

· · · · · · · · · · · · · · · · ·

Monday 1st

Today you will find that communication skills are working at their best. Mundane duties and larger responsibilities work well together. 'Slick' is your middle name, today. If there are any business dealings or career networking to do, then you are sure to get what you want today.

Tuesday 2nd

There is balance and harmony between jobs you must do and those that you would rather not. This is easy to achieve today. It will greatly enhance your career prospects as you show your responsible side to the right people. You could be involved in union disputes. This is a successful day.

Wednesday 3rd

The mood darkens a little as you take a stroll into your relationship sector. It may be time for a sexy interlude or a secret encounter. The desire to satisfy your needs may come at a cost as the Moon sits opposite Uranus in your sign. Two minds may be at odds.

Thursday 4th

Be careful with how you speak to someone special today. Your manipulative, egotistical side may rise. You may wish to get intimate but can be rather selfish now. Work together with a partner to achieve the level of deep intimacy you both require. The other has needs too.

Friday 5th

What are your weekend plans? You're likely to feel the symptoms of a travel bug, today. A weekend getaway sounds just the thing. You wish to explore new places and meet new people. It might be that you must do this alone, as not everyone has the same urges as you. This is not a problem.

Saturday 6th

Today you feel that pressure has lifted. If you have gone off alone, you may find yourself thinking of the past. There is something going on in the background regarding your career or other responsibilities. Keep your ears open, as this will be advantageous to you.

Sunday 7th

As a Taurus, you are possibly the best of the signs for recognising good taste. Today, there is a chance that you will buy something luscious and expensive. This could be for your home or may even be a meal in a quality restaurant. A little devil on your shoulder easily persuades you to do this.

Monday 8th

Back to the working week and you are slightly dreamy. Euphoric feelings are not far away, and you find it hard to concentrate on the job. As no-one is noticing, keep those feelings to yourself and allow yourself to thrive on them a little longer. You deserve it.

Tuesday 9th

Today you have more of a grip on reality and are able to work steadily like a good Taurus. Self-control is easy in the morning hours, but this is not so later in the day. You assert some power and authority where it is not needed. Expect a little blow to your ego.

Wednesday 10th

The Sun burns away the dreamy, surreal feelings you have been having. You may see someone now in a new light. Have you been duped by someone? Were you the one wearing the mask? Paternal or authority figures will feature prominently today. Expect childhood wounds to be exposed.

Thursday 11th

You are probably already planning the weekend. You could be letting off steam with a close friend or a group of friends you trust. This could be on social media too. You are chatty and need to rant. By evening you may begin to feel irritable and needy. Try to calm down.

Friday 12th

If your mood is good, then make this a day or evening with friends. If you are still feeling edgy, then take this time to hunker down with a good book, tasty food and drink, and give yourself some solo time. A fragranced, salt bath will do wonders for your senses.

Saturday 13th

A New Moon in your social sector is a chance to dedicate time to connecting and being more empathic with your friendship groups. This can also make you feel more isolated. There is a risk that you will continue to self-soothe today, but will likely turn to unhealthy vices such as alcohol. Try to find other means of coping.

Sunday 14th

The Moon enters your dreams sector and fires up the mood you are already in. This can take a different slant and will have you making plans or having dreams that are more realistic. Venus and Neptune meet in your social sector, making it a great time to share the love with friends.

Monday 15th

Drawing on skills or lessons learned from the past will be useful now. You are optimistic and see a real way forward to achieving your dream future. This is a time to make solid plans, or at least put them down on paper to look at another time.

Tuesday 16th

You think that you have a tight rein on your emotions. However, someone will come along and hurt your feelings in some way. This may be a big full stop or negative comment about work and travel. As the Moon drifts into your sign around midday, you could be a sulky little bull.

Wednesday 17th

Mercury, the messenger planet, is now in your social sector. He wants you to listen carefully to subtle messages. Dream symbols are important now. You feel somewhat restricted at work today and may need a chat with the boss. Watch that your emotions don't get the better of you.

Thursday 18th

You may be having trouble with authority figures right now. You can be stubborn, as you already know, and this does not help. Make sure that your agenda is in line with your daily responsibilities. Tonight, you just want to feel good about yourself. Let Venus show you how.

Friday 19th

Today you need to network with people. You have many trains of thought and would like some idle chatter. The Moon and Mercury are at odds, so be careful not to be bullish and say something hurtful. Exercise a little self-control with communications today.

Saturday 20th

The Sun is at its balance point today. The equinox asks that you be still and consider this moment before propelling yourself into a new astrological year. You may be emotionally driven towards the future, but you mourn the losses from your past too. Think forwards, it's the only way to go.

Sunday 21st

As your ruler, Venus, enters the home of her lover, Mars, you may feel some anxiety or irritability building up. On the other hand, your sex drive gets a boost. The problem is that you are not in the mood and want to be left alone today. Try to find a balance, if you can.

Monday 22nd

Today you wish to feel nourished by family connections. Phone calls and messages to maternal figures will help. You have plenty to say and it does not hurt to catch up on family gossip. You should be light-hearted and happy today. Everyday conversations are the medicine for you, now.

Tuesday 23rd

Control issues might surface now. There can be thoughts and feelings connected to your parents and your inner child might cry out for attention. Where does nurturing become manipulation? Bear this in mind with your connections today. Let your inner child be your compass. If it feels wrong, it is wrong.

Wednesday 24th

With the Moon now in your family sector, you may unconsciously revert back to your childhood default behaviour patterns. There is a lot of tension going on and harmony is hard to attain. Keep your wits about you and lie low if you need to. Stay safe and grounded.

Thursday 25th

The Sun and Venus are sitting together today. Ego versus self-love will be an issue. This is the time to remind yourself that you must love yourself first. People will stroke your ego, but those same people will leave you standing alone. Try to notice when this is happening.

Friday 26th

Be creative and romantic today. You might feel the drive to get only the beautiful things done. This is a good day for love, and you may even feel the urge to write a poem. You are happy to be there for someone special. This is also the time to have a health check-up.

Saturday 27th

The energy has changed and so has your mood. You get a reality check and can see through an illusion now. Unfortunately, you do not let this pass quietly. You may be aggressive and say what you think without considering consequences. Pause before you act or say anything today.

Sunday 28th

Today's Full Moon will highlight events in your health and duties sector. An ongoing health niggle may be sorted out now. Like the equinox, this Full Moon is about balance and harmony. Look around and see if there is enough of that in your home and work life.

Monday 29th

You are ready to start the working week as everything seems to tick along nicely today. Use this energy to your advantage and work through your 'to do' list. You have the drive, the luck and the attitude to get things done today. You will do a thorough job of all that needs doing.

Tuesday 30th

As the Moon enters your relationship sector you find that you are unable to maintain that good mood. This Moon requires you to pay some attention and make an effort in relationships. Talking about shared dreams and visions can help to lighten the mood and release the pressure.

Wednesday 31st

Deep intimacy is what you are craving now. Your partner might act as a mirror and reflect your deepest feelings. Just be sure that the reflection you are seeing is not your own dark shadow material being projected onto your partner. This can be an intense time, so play it safe.

APRIL

. . . .

Thursday 1st

Today you'll feel more outgoing and may wish to expand your horizons. A controlled urge to explore more in your sex, death and rebirth sector takes over. Access is required to the deeper mysteries of life and you feel inadequate. Higher learning may be on your vision board.

Friday 2nd

There is a lot of lovely energy connecting to the Moon today. You should feel fresh and rejuvenated. Travel and philosophy are on your mind; where would you like to go? Your love of quality has you looking at exotic places to visit. This may be in the form of documentaries.

Saturday 3rd

As the Moon enters your travel house, you sit down and seriously ponder the possibility of foreign travel. You will have some inner resistance as you feel a sense of duty to your commitments. Do not listen to your inner critic, listen to your inner guru and evaluate the lesson.

Sunday 4th

Mercury flies into your dreams sector and urges you to get that vision board sorted. At the moment, you want to keep your plans to yourself, is this because you lack confidence? Venus makes you feel that you should stay home and work on making that a richer experience.

Monday 5th

A conflict arises from within you. You want to point the finger at others for controlling you but have not looked at where you are restricting yourself. This afternoon you are more focused on work, but the mind chatter is still there. Let it babble on – it will soon go.

Tuesday 6th

Do you feel victimised today? The Moon makes some awkward connections to Uranus and Saturn, meaning that there can be a conflict coming from outside. Bosses and authority figures appear to be gunning for you. Your sensitive side feels this, and your ego hates it.

Wednesday 7th

Problems at work may be resolved today and you have a more peaceful time. Stresses can appear to be bigger than they actually are, so you must note how you respond to irritations and ask yourself if your behaviour is necessary. Do not be paranoid or beat yourself up for nothing.

Thursday 8th

You wish to have the company of friends and social groups who will make you feel good. Running with the pack seems a good idea for now and takes the focus off you. Hook up with people who have a spiritual side and learn from them. Find your Zen.

Friday 9th

Is it so difficult for you to learn to relax for a long period? You can easily drift off into fantasy land and get sucked into other's enthusiasm, but is it really you? You are torn between standing out or blending in today. Try having some time alone.

Saturday 10th

Your dream life can be very busy, and this is where you discover what your hopes and wishes are. This should be an easier day, as you are used to this energy. Venus and Jupiter make a helpful connection between work and dreams. Use the energy from these two well-wishing planets wisely.

Sunday 11th

You will experience head versus heart battles today. Mercury and the Moon, representing the mind and emotions respectively, meet up and try to find a happy medium. Listen to what Mercury is telling you through dreams and symbols and then apply emotional experience to achieve peace and harmony.

Monday 12th

A New Moon in Aries acts like another starting point to set intentions and goals for the year. The Moon meeting Venus adds a feminine touch. You will see a softer side of yourself. However, there may be a power struggle between your future dreams and actual travel plans. Venus, as Warrior Goddess, can be quite forceful today.

Tuesday 13th

The Moon enters your own sign and you feel better about yourself. Be warned though, when a Taurus is on top form there is a tendency to be bullish and narcissistic. Do not cross males in authority today as you will get yourself into trouble. Expect the unexpected.

Wednesday 14th

You may have another run-in with a boss, teacher or male relative today. Venus is at the final degree of Aries and, before she comes home, she is asking you to put down your weapons. Aim to be the peace-keeper today and hand out an olive branch if you need to.

Thursday 15th

Venus puts her feet up in her own home for a while. This is your chance to concentrate on balancing your finances and beautifying your home. You will tend to over-spend now, so be very careful. Venus can help bring in the money so maybe you can start a saving pot.

Friday 16th

The Moon contacts a point which deals with destiny. This happens every month and for this year it happens in your money, value and worth sector. Networking and making personal connections are how you will attract those into your life. Think about that when you can today.

Saturday 17th

Your siblings, or those who you think of as such, may come into focus now. Is there a family event going on this weekend? There is a lot of uneasy energy up there today, so you had better watch your step. Do not go into the proverbial china shop unless you are covered in bubble wrap. Filter your speech.

Sunday 18th

The Moon in Cancer has your taste buds drooling for comfort foods. Mothers and maternal love are available for you to access today. Mercury is busy in the heat of the Sun and is unlikely to say anything he regrets. Rest easy and enjoy a nurturing day.

Monday 19th

The Sun jumps into your sign today so this is your birthday month. Happy Birthday! Mercury also comes in. This next month will be warm and lively. Expect many social engagements or a lot of networking and passing of information. Be careful not to gossip or make it all about you.

Tuesday 20th

Today may feel a little too smothering for your liking. You do love a family get together, but there comes a point when it gets too much for you. Before you bite your tongue too much, make a polite exit and regain a sense of self.

Wednesday 21st

Expressing yourself comes easily now. You are almost bursting with joy. You can allow your inner child to come out and play and maybe invite just one or two family members around. You can be the centre of attention within the family. Make them proud and don't be too loud.

Thursday 22nd

If you can put away the checklist or miss an appointment at the gym, this can be a romantic day. Love need not be methodical, it has no rules or check-lists. Mars at the critical degree of your money and worth sector asks if there is anything you have overlooked here.

Friday 23rd

Venus meets up with Uranus today in your sign. This can mean that hot sex is on the cards or a great big bust up. This depends on how you play it. Mars entering your family sector would prefer the former after a nice home-cooked meal.

Saturday 24th

You might struggle to get a grip on reality today. Emotions can seem a little foggy and hide issues you would rather not deal with. By the time evening comes, you will feel irritable and irrational. There is a chance that conflict could arise and you'll fail to keep your thoughts to yourself.

Sunday 25th

The Moon in your health and duties sector asks you to look at what needs balancing in this area. Have you neglected something here? Venus and Mercury meet for a brief chat in your own sign, so expect a little self-talk about how you love and nurture yourself.

Monday 26th

Your internal engine is revved up today. You seek time with a loved one to discuss the meaning of life and maybe have a deeper connection with each other. This evening can be super sexy with harmonic intimacy. Pluto, the control freak, tries to butt in but fails.

Tuesday 27th

A Full Moon in your relationship sector can highlight all that is right and wrong with your special relationships. It is more likely to be what is wrong as this Moon opposes Mercury and Venus in your sign. You could feel selfish and resentful. This is your shadow talking.

Wednesday 28th

Pluto now turns retrograde. This could stir up a whole heap of trouble if you plan on making long excursions this year. As the ruler of your opposite sign, this could also affect your relationships. Use this time to hunt for the lead to transform into gold.

Thursday 29th

Here you have another opportunity to consider higher education or religious studies. Travel may be disrupted, but there is nothing stopping you learning about new cultures from the comfort of your home. Books, maps and documentaries can scratch that itch. Exotic foods can also satisfy the taste for the foreign.

Friday 30th

Today, as the Sun meets Uranus, be mindful that any weird ideas you have could actually be tangible. This is ego and the unusual meeting up. You may even think you are a genius. Hold that thought, it could be worth something. Alternatively, you might want to start a revolution.

MAY

· · · · · · · · · · · · · · · · ·

Saturday 1st

There is powerful energy around today. It is easy to keep
emotions out of anything you do now. The air is electric
and you will feel on top of the world. This could be just a
mountaintop, but today you feel seen and heard. You are in
top form.

Sunday 2nd

Venus and Neptune make helpful connections to the Moon
in your travel sector. You could be seeing things from a new
perspective and feeling drawn to making improvements.
Venus in your own sign is bringing in the money while
Neptune reminds you that your dreams are possible now.

Monday 3rd

As the Moon dips into your career sector at the start of the
week, you may feel a little off-balance. Your high from the
weekend is now being opposed by those above you. Try to be
subtle and not bullish about any plans you wish to discuss
with others.

Tuesday 4th

Today you must consider the consequences of any new,
radical plans you have made in your head. Perhaps you
have not been given the go-ahead and will have to wait for
approval. This may feel more personal than it really is, but
that is the way you take it.

Wednesday 5th

Once more you have to listen to authority figures. Jupiter is visited by the Moon in your career sector and this signifies a meeting with a boss, guru or otherwise beneficial person. Jupiter only wants the best for you but warns not to get in over your head.

Thursday 6th

There is something that needs completion in the workplace before you can move on. Find some empathy today and connect with others. You might feel things are dissolving around you, but this is just a momentary feeling and will soon pass. Play nicely and keep control of your emotions today.

Friday 7th

By midday, you are fired up in your dream world. Plans are likely to run through your head faster than you can get them down on paper. You are back in control of your own inner world and may have some money-making schemes going on. You look forward to the weekend.

Saturday 8th

The Moon connects to Mercury and allows you mental capacities to bring you clarity. However, the Moon also makes a poor connection to Mars and you may get a little aggressive. Watch that you are not getting too big for your boots. There is a chance you will overspend today.

Sunday 9th

Venus leaves your own sign and moves into your money and home sector. There will be plenty of networking with women or lovers over the next few weeks. You may feel slightly manipulated today but this may be paranoia so do nothing, be mindful and let this feeling pass.

Monday 10th

The Moon is now in your own sign and you might feel self-righteous. There will be no stopping you from saying what you feel today; just be sure not to act out. The Moon in Taurus every month connects with Uranus and this is when you might just blow your top.

Tuesday 11th

Today, a New Moon in your sign gives you the opportunity to set goals and intentions around what you want for yourself. Be realistic and think of how self-improvement and empowerment can help. You have a tendency to be selfish now, this is not good for your personal New Moon.

Wednesday 12th

Today is a day of networking and sharing your ideas. You are in a better frame of mind to take these higher up and showcase your vision for the future. When the day is done, you need a romantic evening or a great meal. Perhaps a midweek date is on the cards.

Thursday 13th

The planet of truth, justice and expansion is about to leave your work sector. Are there any loose ends that you need to tie up today? Mercury and the point of destiny are both visited by the Moon and you have a great chance of stepping up your game.

Friday 14th

Jupiter will now be in your social sector for around a year. This is great for making connections with unusual people or organisations. There is a good chance that you will find your soul tribe during this time. Your friendship groups will greatly expand while Jupiter is here.

Saturday 15th

This weekend you may have to make a lot of short trips or catch up with family members. This is all good, as there may be some tasty meals involved and this will satisfy your inner child. You feel loved, nurtured and nourished, so remember to give back what you receive.

Sunday 16th

You are emotionally driven today. Be careful, as the Moon meeting Mars could mean that you have tantrums or act the bully. This is very likely to come from childhood wounds and you are being triggered. Note them for what they are and nurture your inner child selflessly.

Monday 17th

Are you still sulking in the corner? Have your feelings been hurt today? You may feel powerless as Moon sits opposite Pluto who likes to control things. However, the Sun also connects to Pluto today and will show you how you are conditioned to react when these uncomfortable situations arise.

Tuesday 18th

When you are in good form, you are a great leader. You can be head of a family or the one in charge of family events. People look to you, so do not let them down and get stroppy today. Saturn is asking that you take responsibility seriously and show your worth.

Wednesday 19th

As the Moon now opposes Jupiter, you may see issues come up regarding friendship groups. There is a possibility that you feel left out or ignored. On the other hand, this is another area where you can lead positively, but can also be prone to sulking if you do not get your own way.

Thursday 20th

You're likely to try to be creative, romantic or playful today, but may find that your heart is just not in it. Is this because you are being too formal and not letting yourself go? The Sun has now left your sign and is shining on your money, possessions and worth sector.

Friday 21st

A conflict of interests has you torn between your head and your heart today. You are not usually led by emotions as you prefer a solid foundation, but today something disintegrates. This could be a former idea or plan. Sit still, all may not be lost just yet.

Saturday 22nd

Please check in with your health today, particularly your blood pressure. Mercury and Neptune are squaring off and you can no longer tell fact from fiction. Aim to put all your cards on the table and find balance, or else something will probably suffer. This is likely to be your health.

Sunday 23rd

The planet which teaches us about responsibility, hard work and introspection goes retrograde today. You will feel its effects in your career. This can be a frustrating time where you have no choice but to toe the line. You may feel emotionally trapped. This will pass, but Saturn's lessons will last a few months.

Monday 24th

Turning your attention towards your relationships will help to calm you, today. You may still feel tense but focusing on a significant other should help to take the edge off. Any important relationships, including those with older people you admire, will be beneficial to you today.

Tuesday 25th

The Moon makes its first contact to retrograde Saturn. Remember that this will affect your work sector. You may be digging too deep for information or exerting too much control. You will feel as if you could take this on and win, but be cautious; Saturn is retrograde for many months. This bravado will soon pass.

Wednesday 26th

Today there is a Full Moon in your house of sex, death and rebirth. This will highlight that something has come to a natural end or completion. You will also see themes of travel and exploration illuminated now. What has come full circle in the last six months?

Thursday 27th

Coming off the back of the Full Moon is a lot of tension. Networking, commerce, finances and value are all hard to juggle today. Everything seems to be surrounded by fog and just out of your reach. Leave it there. Get your head down and concentrate on something tangible for now.

. . . .

Friday 28th

The energy shifts and so does your mood. You are ready for the weekend and maybe even planning a trip. You should now feel more optimistic and connect with friends for some weekend fun. Outdoor activities are favoured under this energy, so get out there and climb a mountain this weekend.

Saturday 29th

That old trickster planet, Mercury, goes retrograde again today. This time he will do this in your finance and worth sector. He sits with Venus before doing so. As your ruler, she asks him to go easy on you but still heed the usual warnings. Watch your words, travel and technology.

Sunday 30th

This weekend has refreshed and rejuvenated you. You feel perfectly balanced within. Do not take this for granted, but use this space to enjoy just being you. Friendships tick along nicely and your mood is generally optimistic and cheery. Have a lovely light-hearted day.

Monday 31st

Monday starts with your mind on the job in hand and you bring your good mood to work. There may be an occasion to speak to the boss and this is favoured by some energy, regardless of Mercury retrograde. Keep it simple today; overcomplicating things will spoil that great mood of yours.

JUNE

....

Tuesday 1st

You find it easy to share dreams and visions with your social groups. Today you can dream big and have the potential to make many connections. Joining a protest rally or signing up to support a good cause will make you feel great. Your ego inflates, but not without reason. You may be onto something huge.

Wednesday 2nd

Do you feel like you are at a crossroads? This is a moment to pause and reflect before taking action. You may be wondering if you have done the right thing and have a crisis of conscience. Speak to people who nurture and support you. Keep moving on.

Thursday 3rd

Your ruler has just moved into your communications sector and will bring with her some harmony. This is just what you need to ride this Mercury retrograde. You feel sociable but, when evening comes, you will want to switch off and enjoy your own company. You have had enough of people today.

Friday 4th

Who in your social circle is about to be exposed? Let it not be you. Mercury asks you to re-consider certain friendships. You are happy enough doing your own thing today. Whatever lights your fire, do it. This can be a soul-refreshing time so make the most of it.

Saturday 5th

You might be party to some aggravation today. The tense energy around is edgy and uneasy. You will see control issues around work and family. People may try to coerce you into socialising but all you need is a good book or TV show. Let others make their own messes.

Sunday 6th

As the Moon enters your sign, you will feel justified in having spent so much time alone this weekend. You may notice that your mood and energy are balanced, and you are ready to start the week in good spirits. You may have some good luck or simply enjoy good food and drink.

Monday 7th

The monthly meet up between Moon and Uranus occurs today. You feel this like an electric shock running through you. You can either come up with some genius, inspired ideas or act out unexpectedly. Make sure you can separate the real from fantasy now as this could present a problem.

Tuesday 8th

Today you manage to get a firmer grip on your finances. Mars and Pluto, both rulers of your opposite sign deal with joint finances. Take today to look at where you are invested with another person or group. You may be able to claim back what is yours.

Wednesday 9th

Listen very carefully to subtle messages, now. The communication network is buzzing with activity and you may learn something to your advantage. Bosses and leaders are the people to connect with. Remember that Mercury is still retrograde, so you will have to sort out information which is useful or not.

Thursday 10th

A New Moon in your finance sector is a great time to think about investments or putting your spending to a worthy cause. Just think about this for now. Wait until Mercury, the planet of commerce, is back on track before you act. Do not be fooled by tricksters or conmen.

Friday 11th

Today Mercury is in the heat of the Sun. At this time, he gets new downloads of information or a new mission. Say nothing but take on board anything you may learn from an elder. Feed your soul with home comforts, favourite foods and family life. Today has fortunate energy for you to access.

Saturday 12th

Mars comes marching into your family sector; his outspoken directness may upset people at this time. You will want to be the star of your own show when Mars is here. Today the Moon and Venus have a lady's night in your communications sector. Perhaps give your mum a call.

Sunday 13th

You may come across control issues today. The Moon in your family sector has opposed Pluto already and this will feel like a struggle between nurture and nature. Mothers and fathers will be in focus. As the Moon then sits with Mars, it is likely to stir up some trouble.

Monday 14th

Do you feel edgy and restricted today? Are you digging your heels in and refusing to budge? This is your childhood instinct kicking in and not the response of an adult. You may want to take a good look at where your behaviour is coming from.

Tuesday 15th

A very difficult connection between Saturn retrograde in your career sector and Uranus in your sign may see a conflict at work. You may erupt violently today. Restriction of your freedom makes you angry and you are not slow to tell people. Watch your words, you never know who is listening.

Wednesday 16th

You continue to express yourself today. Make sure that what you are saying is true and check all your facts. Mercury will have a field day if Taurus goes shouting their mouth off unguarded today. Try to lie low until this feeling passes and bite your tongue if you have to.

Thursday 17th

Seeking solace in romance may not be the ideal answer to recent tensions. It is possible that a love interest will be seen through rose coloured glasses. This will not be fair on them when the glasses come off and you are dissatisfied with their human flaws.

Friday 18th

Try to get more of a level head before the weekend arrives. Look to mundane duties and helping others to make you feel more grounded. Put your energy into going to the gym or doing some other exercise like yoga. A walk in nature should help you too.

Saturday 19th

Mercury is going to turn direct again now; this was a heavy retrograde for your finances and self-worth. Now is the time to slow down and re-visit all those places where you acted out under Mercury's influence. Love is not favoured today as you have your own needs to take care of.

Sunday 20th

The Moon slips into your relationship sector but makes bad connections to this sign's rulers. You can try your best to wine and dine a loved one, but prepare to be disappointed. Put that date on hold and re-schedule for a better time. Jupiter also goes retrograde today.

Monday 21st

Today is the Summer Solstice, the longest day of the year. If you can, make the most of this super-charged sun energy by enjoying a sultry evening with someone special. Sparks may fly but they do not have to be bad ones. This is a great time to make magic together as love and dreams are in sync.

Tuesday 22nd

Mercury turns direct today. Communications will be easier, and you can now sign off any deals. Wandering and exploring new territories attracts you. This could also be done with deep, philosophical conversations with the right people. Those who help you grow beyond your comfort zone are the ones to seek.

Wednesday 23rd

You may have to take another look at financial transactions that stretched you during the retrograde. This is a day where money is highlighted as Venus (your own money) sits opposite Pluto (shared money). Double check any agreements or joint investments made recently. This could cause you some grief.

Thursday 24th

Today there is a Full Moon in your travel sector. A plan for a trip away may come together now or you may already be away. You could be called upon to organise a trip as you excel in this area. Your leadership skills are highlighted under this Full Moon.

Friday 25th

The planet of dreams and illusions goes retrograde today. Neptune is in your social sector and for you, this means that friendship groups can be dissolved or individuals within them will be exposed as fake. Sacrifices will be made during this time, you may feel lost at sea.

Saturday 26th

You have more control of things today. Those financial worries are now being solved. There may be a small personal loss, but a joint venture is now at peace. Venus is at the end of her stay in your communications sector, perhaps she has balanced the books while there.

Sunday 27th

In your career sector, you may have to deal with out-of-hours business which you will likely resent. You may have overlooked something important and be spending your weekend time catching up. Put your responsible hat on and let irritability bubble under the surface. Motivation will get this done today.

Monday 28th

Progress at work is slow and steady. Networking across organisations and groups will take up most of the day. This is a positive day, things get done and you receive recognition from those above you. Well done, this is you at your best, determined and motivated to do something well.

Tuesday 29th

You may already be looking forward to the weekend. Time spent on social media connecting with like-minded people should bring satisfaction today. Sometimes you like to remain anonymous, but there are times when merging with a group makes you happier. Today is very likely to be one of those days. You take on new ideas now.

Wednesday 30th

The sociable Moon is making you think a great deal. Fresh perspectives may be difficult to get your head around but, if you take your time, you can accept them. This is the first of the coming days where you are asked to self-sacrifice. Let old habits die, now.

JULY

· · · · · · · · · · · · · · · · ·

Thursday 1st

Today you simply must play by the rules. You may well come across as aggressive, bullish and unhelpful, even if that isn't your intention. Mars is in your family sector and makes you act out like a child who wants their own way. Unfortunately, you will come up against powerful authority figures.

Friday 2nd

Lick your wounds. You can stomp around all you like, but today you must retreat and take time out. When you have sufficiently grounded yourself, you will begin to see reason and get back on track with being an adult. A fiery Moon in your dreams sector has caused the need for this.

Saturday 3rd

By afternoon you will be a typical Taurus and need to surround yourself with nice things. You may consider spending and spoiling yourself. Getting out in nature and enjoying a more sensory experience will be far more beneficial. Nature is beautiful and as the astrological gardener, you will enjoy it.

Sunday 4th

You will still feel edgy inside and the Moon in your sign makes a poor connection to your ruler Venus. There is something creative or inventive waiting to emerge from you; perhaps you do not know what it is yet. Sit with it – it will be worth the wait.

Monday 5th

The muddy waters of Neptune retrograde are being stirred up.
Take extra care to connect with the right people, as it will be
all too easy to be swept away by false gurus and inauthentic
leaders now. Find something to hold on to; you have a precious
new passion awaiting its birth.

Tuesday 6th

You have the desire to talk and exchange ideas with people.
This is juxtaposed by wanting to keep your ideas to yourself.
Maybe this is a time where you just listen. Remember to be
on the lookout for falsities. If it seems too good to be true, it
probably isn't.

Wednesday 7th

Drive, desire and responsibility are all looking good today. You
manage to find a balance between home and work, although it
will seem hard at first and perhaps needs some perseverance.
Emotionally, you are in a good space and enjoy chatting and
researching. You may also be making short visits today.

Thursday 8th

At some point today, find time for yourself and clear your
head of all unnecessary thoughts. Listen to what your heart is
telling you now. You will have to sift through some driftwood
brought up by Neptune, but clarity will come. You will wish to
feel nurtured by clear thinking today.

Friday 9th

You will be surprised by conversations with your family. 'Mother's wisdom' is called that for a reason. Chat to female elders or tap into your inner nurturer. Intuition is strong today and may come as a bolt of lightning. You will wonder why you have never thought of something before.

Saturday 10th

A New Moon in your communications sector asks you to make positive affirmations regarding women, mothers, your dreams and intuition. You may now feel protective of someone. It is more likely that your inner child is guarding a new passion that they are not ready to share yet.

Sunday 11th

There is no stopping you today. You are creative and expressive. It could be that you are the star of the show at a family gathering. An elder tries to dumb you down. Be nice, they may just be showing concern. Mercury flies into your communication sector with love.

Monday 12th

You have both Mars and Venus in your family sector. This could be perfect family relating or meeting your future family. Watch this space. The Moon passes both of them today and, if you feel a little desirous, this could be why. Express these desires now while the energy is favourable. Mercury will help here too.

Tuesday 13th

Mars and Venus meet up today at the same degree. This is
hot stuff. You should make a move on someone special. Greet
them, treat them and have an all-out great time. As a Taurus,
you will know how to make the most of this special time.

Wednesday 14th

The Moon has passed to your creative sector. Mars and Venus
are still together. Maybe you have found your muse. There is a
chance that you are star-struck with someone who has recently
crossed your path. Alternatively, you may already be asking for
their credentials.

Thursday 15th

Neptune is the one to watch today. In a connection to the Sun,
you see muddy water ahead but opposition to the Moon means
that you could not care less. You may already be caught in a
love trap. Use your Taurean energy and get more grounded.
You need a reality check.

Friday 16th

Duty calls. Your heart has been racing lately but now you
realise that, joking aside, you may need to schedule some
health checks. Time to knuckle down, get to the gym and
make sure your obligations are fulfilled. Have your fun but do
not forget your responsibilities.

. . . .

Saturday 17th

This weekend you have a need to get to know someone deeper. By evening you could be seduced by the Moon in your relationship sector. This phase also tends to bring out your shadow side. If you do not want this to happen just yet, be aware of where you are projecting.

Sunday 18th

Be sure not to push through someone's boundaries today. You might like to go beyond your comfort zone, but your partner or significant other may not. It is possible that you both like to stretch but in different directions. This could lead to some unnecessary tension.

Monday 19th

Do you really want an intimate experience with a person or with the external world? Your shadow, or indeed your partner, prefers to explore the deeper mysteries of life whereas you like to know how far you can go. It is not easy to find that happy medium now.

Tuesday 20th

Well done, you managed to respect another's wishes. Today you seek excitement in the wider world. Both Saturn and Uranus recognise your need for exploration and new horizons. Making travel plans or watching documentaries will be good for your soul and scratch that itch. You may go far in your imagination.

Wednesday 21st

As the Moon moves into your travel sector tonight, it also connects nicely to Venus and Mars. Your desires and drive to acquire those desires are in sync with your heart. There is a way to explore and push boundaries without hurting anyone. A long-haul trip may just be on the cards.

Thursday 22nd

Venus glides into your creative sector. This area also deals with falling in love and expressing your needs. You could be making grand gestures as Venus opposes Jupiter, who makes everything he touches bigger. If you must do this, make sure you can back it up later.

Friday 23rd

What can you transform, transmute or get rid of completely? The Moon's monthly visit to Pluto asks that you de-clutter and recycle. This can be anything from material things to deeper unconscious issues that you need to deal with in order to grow as a person.

Saturday 24th

Your career sector is lit up by a Full Moon today. What has come to completion recently? Think back over the last six months for a clue. Now is the time to strip back anything that is stopping this from showing its full potential. You may have to be strict with yourself or with someone else.

Sunday 25th

Mars sitting opposite the Moon makes it difficult for you to be focused today. You may feel edgy and emotional but also like the proverbial bull in the ring. You do not like being told what to do today. Calm down, walk away from the tension and do some controlled breathing.

Monday 26th

You feel more sociable and empathic today. Merging with someone special is important now. A cuddle may be all you need to feel part of something good. You may seek out your wisest friend and fill your soul with good advice. Try not to inflate your ego at this time.

Tuesday 27th

When in your social sector, the Moon makes contact with Neptune. This can influence your senses and you may drift off into a fantasy world. Remember that Neptune is retrograde and all is not as it seems right now. Stay real and watch out for deceivers, liars and sycophants.

Wednesday 28th

Jupiter backs his way into your career sector. Usually, he is a good luck charm but in retrograde, he asks you to go over something you once thought was fortunate but is not so now. He could also be exposing an injustice at work. Chatty Mercury flies into your family sector.

Thursday 29th

Be sure to check out what Jupiter is exposing at work. He now sits opposite Mars and things might get a little aggressive. Put your extra energy into your creative endeavours or say it as it is, no holds barred. After that, you may want to retreat and be alone.

Friday 30th

Are you hiding under the bedclothes today? This is fine if you are in the right. If you have any guilt, then you must face the music. By evening, all eyes will be on you. Usually you would love this, but not today; you would rather be alone.

Saturday 31st

The Moon in your sign makes uneasy connections to Mercury and Saturn. This may suggest that you have been involved in an argument with an elder or boss. Own up, do the right thing or this weekend may be a total waste. Your ruler, Venus, helps you restore harmony.

AUGUST

....

Sunday 1st

Mercury is in the heart of the Sun and connecting to harsh Saturn who sits in your career sector. You begrudge having to deal with work issues at the weekend. This is necessary. Take any advice or constructive criticism the way it is meant. You are likely to erupt in temper today.

Monday 2nd

You are still feeling the pinch from the conflict in the workplace. Your leadership qualities will be questioned. Ego battles need to be sorted by the weekend. Jupiter sits at the critical degree of your career sector. This could be a make-or-break time in work.

Tuesday 3rd

Today should be somewhat easier. There is softer energy and communication becomes easier. Money matters will need a review. At this point in time, you would be wise to follow your heart's yearnings and look to creating a future which suits you.

Wednesday 4th

Sift through information offered to you now. Not all is relevant or helpful. You may have to let some of your hopes and dreams go. Look at what is impossible or irrational. By evening you will want to be nurtured, even if that is just by treating yourself to a nice meal.

Thursday 5th

Trips or messages to family help you come back to a good place. Doing what you can to help others relaxes you and makes you feel good again. Get a health check-up or relieve some tension with a visit to the gym or a brisk walk in nature.

Friday 6th

There is still an underlying ripple of angst within you. Your ego has taken a bashing and needs soothing. Let someone take care of you this weekend. Getting away may not be possible, but losing yourself in a different environment could do wonders. Surprise yourself with something unusual.

Saturday 7th

As the Moon moves into your family sector, you may wish to visit loved ones. Go back to childhood, laugh and be the family clown or golden child. Take time today to let your inner child play without a filter. You need to express yourself in a safe place. Allow yourself this moment in the spotlight.

Sunday 8th

Today, a New Moon in your family sector gives you a boost and helps you set some intentions. You are still feeling disturbed about events at work. Be honest with yourself and look at where you could have been at fault and acted better. Integrity is everything to you. Do not let yourself down.

Monday 9th

How much chatter going on in your head is self-talk? Today your mind will not be quiet. Listen carefully to what you are telling yourself. You may come up against opposition from a boss or leader. Check every detail before communicating both in speech and written word. Avoid unnecessary judgements.

Tuesday 10th

Cool down, you could be getting hot and irritated again. Your ruler, Venus, is asking that you use this energy wisely and do some physical exercise. You can also appease this state of unrest by getting on with your daily routine in a methodical way. Mundane jobs can help now.

Wednesday 11th

The Moon meets Venus and they have an emotional heart to heart in your creative sector. The consensus is that you must look after your health right now. Emotional and physical strain are taking their toll. You feel defeated but cannot rest. Gentle exercise or a long bath will help.

Thursday 12th

You may have found more of a balance now between work and home duties. Mercury has just entered your creative sector and will help you say what you feel with meaning. Negotiations will be easier now, but you must take care to check all the details before responding.

Friday 13th

Right now, you have more of a sense of what is just and fair. You are able to look at all sides of a dispute and not just the side that serves your interests. There may be some tweaking to do with shared resources. This could make you slightly uncomfortable.

Saturday 14th

Spend time with a special person or someone you admire today; you have much to learn from them. These lessons can show you where your triggers are and, if you pay attention, this will enhance your personal growth. Today can be a romantic and even sexy day if you allow another to lead the way.

Sunday 15th

Today can go in two different directions. If you let ego get in the way, there will be trouble. If, however, you can find your sensitive side, you will have a seductive and sensual day. The choice is yours: tension and rows or sweetness and love.

Monday 16th

Deep feelings and needs stir you up today. This can lead to you saying the wrong thing and pushing other's boundaries. You want to stretch your own limits, and this is fine, but you may go too far. Travel and exploration may be on your mind now. Foreign lands call.

Tuesday 17th

You yearn to go away and discover new territory but right now this seems out of your reach. Researching unknown lands or cultures can satisfy that itch. Exploring the mysteries of life and death with someone you trust can bring fascinating conversations. Higher education is also something to consider now.

Wednesday 18th

Thoughts and feelings from yesterday become larger now. You have wandered off in your mind and planning trips and itineraries for travel purposes. Today you feel as if you could conquer the world. Weigh up your duties and obligations and make time for some of this travel you are craving.

Thursday 19th

Uranus, who has been in your sign for two years, goes retrograde today. This earth-shaking planet can move mountains for you and help you progress, but in retrograde he could bring a landslide down on your plans. Mercury and Mars meet up and discuss a new fitness regime for you.

Friday 20th

A lot of mixed energy today can give you knee-jerk reactions. You may feel blocked and restricted at one turn and then feel free and expressive at the next. Let these feelings come and go and note what triggers them. The workplace will be buzzing with activity and you must stay alert.

Saturday 21st

Are you feeling rebellious? You may feel like quitting your job or starting a revolution. This is just a fleeting phase of the Moon. While you are in this mood, try doing something spontaneous for the greater good such as an act of charity or sticking up for someone.

Sunday 22nd

A Full Moon at the critical degree of your work sector will show exactly what has been covertly going on at work. Make a mental note of it but do not let it spoil your weekend. Use today to merge and connect with your tribe. This will be beneficial to you.

Monday 23rd

The Moon in your social sector can make you more outgoing. However, an opposition to Mars in your creative sector can make you argumentative again. An easy connection between Venus and Saturn makes sure that balance is maintained at work and all jobs get done.

Tuesday 24th

You are inclined to drift away and day-dream today. You may find that something you previously thought solid is now dissolving or perhaps even no longer exists. There is a chance for you to transform an old, outdated way of thinking and get a new perspective. Listen carefully to subliminal messages.

Wednesday 25th

Your dreams and visions are fired up now and waiting to be manifested. Spending time alone and mulling over these will be good for you. You may feel a little selfish today. Someone needs your attention, but you are not ready or prepared to listen. You stubbornly refuse to see another's point of view.

Thursday 26th

Pluto seems to be restricting your inner vision now. He likes to control things or force endings and beginnings. A helpful connection to Jupiter makes you see that this is not a bad thing. Your dreams get bigger and plans begin to take shape. Pluto asks you to leave something behind.

Friday 27th

The Moon enters your sign this morning and your needs turn inwards. You may come up against an authority figure and this will put a slight dampener on the day. Overall, this is an easier day than most. Make the most if it, the weekend is here.

Saturday 28th

When the Moon is in your sign, it meets up with temperamental Uranus. This means that volatile emotions are not far away. Fear not; your ruler, Venus, is making a soft connection to Uranus. A lovely surprise could be the trigger of those emotions today. Enjoy the surprises.

Sunday 29th

You have more control and more sense of how you might manifest some of your dreams. Your mental, emotional and practical faculties are all working together. Do not over-think or burn yourself out as this energy is too good to mess up. Keep it simple.

Monday 30th

Make your finances a priority today. Check all your accounts and look to where money is being leaked unnecessarily. You might discover old subscriptions that you are paying for but no longer need. Mercury in your health and duties sector will sniff these out for you. He likes to balance your books.

Tuesday 31st

The Moon in your money and value sector acts as an anchor between Mars in your creative sector and Neptune in your social sector. Now is the time to review where your time, energy and finances go. You must look at your healthy and not-so-healthy habits today.

SEPTEMBER

. . . .

Wednesday 1st

You will need to watch what you say today. The Moon and Mercury are squaring off. Your emotions may be too close to the surface. The energy requires that you take care of your own needs. This is easily done by filling your stomach and tantalising your senses with some good food.

Thursday 2nd

Today you can use your intuition and tap into some genius thinking. Here may be a way of doing something that you have not previously considered. Try not to spend too much time alone as there is a danger of self-medicating or relying on unhealthy habits.

Friday 3rd

Your get up and go gets a boost from Mars and you can express yourself well now. There may be some opposition from family members. Your dreams are easier to access, and you can cut through any illusions with ease. Take care with controlling people; you may want to lead but someone else has other ideas.

Saturday 4th

Today the Moon makes difficult connections to Saturn and Uranus. This could restrict your movement or self-expression. You have the gift of the gab today but there are elders who may not like what you have to say. Do not rise to it, this will soon pass.

Sunday 5th

With the Moon in your family sector, you can enjoy the natural audience you receive from them. Be careful that this does not turn into showing off and becoming a bore. You have a tendency to over-inflate your role in the family and luck may not be on your side.

Monday 6th

You may find that you are at a standstill today. Reclaiming skills you have learned in the past could propel you into the future, but you are not there yet. Your ruler is not in a good connection with Pluto, who likes to transform things, so now is not the time to act.

Tuesday 7th

A New Moon in your creative sector asks you to consider what projects you would like to excel in. How much effort do you need to put in? This is also a favourable time for a new love affair to begin. A boost from Mars will give you the drive and staying power you need.

Wednesday 8th

The Moon shifts into your health and duties sector. You must look at how balanced these areas are. Are you allowing yourself enough time for leisure? Check in with your health right now, perhaps you can fit in an extra session at the gym.

Thursday 9th

You have no problem saying what you feel today, although you run the risk of being rather controlling with it. The Moon's influence today asks you to take the kinder route. Listen to what your body needs and take more control with that.

Friday 10th

Venus and the Moon have an early morning meet-up before the Moon moves into your relationship sector. Venus moves there shortly after. This indicates a sexy weekend where you can have quality time with someone special. Alternatively, you could be working on your own shadow and learning to love your darker side.

Saturday 11th

Your relationship times are always explosive one way or another. When the Moon is there, it sits opposite volatile Uranus, which can mean either rows and tension or explosive sex. There are other favourable connections now which indicate that the better option is more likely.

Sunday 12th

There is a dilemma now and you may struggle between finding time for friends or a lover. You have the energy to do both, so why not? Doing the right thing by both parties can be easily done if you so wish. This evening is more favourable for intimacy with a lover.

Monday 13th

Even though you desire to learn about other cultures and philosophies, you find it difficult to change your mindset. You can wander afar in your own head but not always in the right direction. Drifting too far away from truth and more to your own agenda does not help you to grow.

113

Tuesday 14th

The Sun burns away some illusions you have been having. You may see more clearly now. This concerns your social groups and friendships. Liars and cheats may be exposed. You feel angry about this and need to see justice in some way. You dislike the harmony being upset in your tribe.

Wednesday 15th

Mars enters your health and duties sector now. This will give you an incredible boost in those areas. You will see your energy increase and your drive to get things done will be on fire. Mars will ensure that you have the time and energy to enjoy all your routines.

Thursday 16th

You have the ability to bring something up from the depths of your being and transform it. You may be a stubborn bull but, when you set your sights on something, there is no stopping you. Most of the day you will be churning up old emotions and discarding them.

Friday 17th

Venus in your opposite sign is the sexy seductress. She squares off with the Moon and Saturn today. You could be seduced over to the dark side in a relationship. As she is also responsible for money, watch that you do not invest unwisely. You may be persuaded to join a financial venture. Be careful.

Saturday 18th

Once again, the Moon is in your social sector at the weekend but not until the evening. She meets with lucky Jupiter, which could mean that you take a chance by going to a social event and it pays off. Jolly Jupiter just wants you to have a bit of fun.

Sunday 19th

Venus shows her softer side now as she connects with the Moon in your social circle. This is a blending of your seductress and mermaid goddess. Perhaps Venus is now a siren and luring you to fantasy land. You will be in for a surprise if you follow her lead, but will it be a good one?

Monday 20th

A Full Moon late tonight brightens up the sky. As it passes by Neptune, you will see false friends fall away. You may come to realise that groups you have joined lately are draining you. Empathic and poetic qualities are strong now. Listen to your dreams tonight.

Tuesday 21st

You allow yourself some time to dream and remember what your personal visions are. Mars gets you all fired up and proactive. You plan where you would like to be in the future and what steps you must take to get there. Be sensible with your imagined time frame.

Wednesday 22nd

The Equinox is here, and the length of day is equal to night. Time stands still before the tipping point into the darker months. Take this time to pause and reflect. Mercury will retrograde again soon, so remember to back up devices and double check travel plans now.

Thursday 23rd

The Sun has settled in your health and duties sector and health issues will get a boost from its vitality. The Moon enters your own sign. You are likely to feel torn between being selfless and selfish. Take a lesson from the equinox and choose balance. Your love life could be volatile today; expect a battle or take cover.

Friday 24th

You feel somewhat emotionally drained. There could be a meltdown coming if you are not careful. You need to retreat and re-charge but cannot seem to find the time. A fuse will blow if you fail to rest and put yourself first. Know your limits – you are not Superman.

Saturday 25th

There is good energy around to support you having some downtime. Saturn allows Mars to get a pit stop in your health and duties sector. The Moon connects to Neptune, giving you the time for a sleepy Saturday under a blanket if this is what you wish for.

Sunday 26th

Another Mercury retrograde begins. Be thankful that you have enjoyed a rest, as this one will cover your health and duties sector. Your health might suffer but think of it as a sign to slow down, which is exactly what Mercury is doing. Review and re-assess this area of your life.

Monday 27th

You may be extra communicative today. Do you really want to tell everyone your most secret dreams and desires? A connection to Neptune may loosen your tongue. This is OK if you talk to someone you trust, just don't overtly advertise your inner world or you may well regret it.

Tuesday 28th

Put your money where your mouth is or keep it shut today. Mercury retrograde will interfere with money matters and self-worth. Do not make any impulse buys for the home. Have an evening of spoiling yourself with good food and wine but do not break the budget.

Wednesday 29th

You are fidgety and fizzy today. The Moon asks that you spend time nourishing yourself or others. A visit to a maternal figure could prove beneficial. Venus adds some love to your social life. Take a midweek break to connect with your tribe. Social media groups can be fun now.

Thursday 30th

There is beautiful energy today. It is all watery and emotional, but it is stable. This is the time to be a little more adaptable to suggestions of others. Your love life, social life and communications are all involved now. Relax and go with the flow today.

OCTOBER

....

Friday 1st

You are already in the mood for the weekend. The current energy lifts your spirits and you may even suggest or attend a party. Connections from the Sun and Mars in your health and duties sector make you feel good. The jobs are done, so now it is time to let your hair down.

Saturday 2nd

You might come up against some opposition from people in charge or elders. You will push on through this and disregard them. A useful connection from your ruler helps you to persuade others to join in the fun. Don't overdo it, as this may make enemies.

Sunday 3rd

Today you may be doing small jobs for people. Offering your services to those in need will win you brownie points. This could just be as simple as some DIY or a selfless act of kindness. People will look up to you today and you won't let them down.

Monday 4th

Expression and creation may be hard to access today. The Moon is eager to help you show the world what you've got but Neptune sitting opposite makes it a little foggy. This could be a day when things simply do not go your way. You may find it hard to make a start, and possibly shouldn't anyway.

Tuesday 5th

This afternoon you make more headway and can look objectively at projects or passions you are involved in. The joy returns and you are able to discern what did not work and transform it. Look at how the balance between work and free time lies. You may need to make changes here.

Wednesday 6th

A New Moon in your health and duties sector allows you to make decisions about the way forward. The Sun and Moon sit with Mars and you may feel emotionally drained or fired up. Use this as a moment to pause and reflect before moving on.

Thursday 7th

Pluto is now direct and likes that you have de-cluttered some areas of your life. Travel plans are now possible again. This evening you are inclined to spend time with a lover or, if single, to spoil yourself with luxuries. Your ruler enters your intimacy sector, so prepare for a sultry time.

Friday 8th

Ego and sex drive are on a high today. You have a need for release or physical exercise. You may not do things by the book today, as you feel a little rebellious. Shadow material could surface from your unconscious for you to deal with. Do not fear it.

Saturday 9th

Friends and lovers clash today. You can't please everyone. This is a difficult day and you need an outlet for your energy. Words of passion or anger need to be checked as this is still Mercury retrograde time and today, he is in the heat of the Sun.

Sunday 10th

Saturn now turns direct and the pressure in your social circle is relieved. People who have been exposed as fake are no longer in your groups. Venus is asking that you explore the width and depth of your close relationships and where you are joined in financial obligations with someone.

Monday 11th

A bit of luck may come your way today as the Moon makes a nice connection to Jupiter. This is likely to be in the workplace but will also be connected to something radical and unusual. Continue to explore the larger world; you may just learn something new.

Tuesday 12th

One step at a time, remember. If you have a metaphorical mountain to climb today, use your knowledge of being an earth sign and be methodical, determined and steady. Progress may feel slow, but you are doing the right thing. Look at all angles and make strong decisions on the way up.

Wednesday 13th

Today is another day where you might recycle an old idea or habit. You can be too fixed in your own theories and find it difficult to accept another. The planetary energy is here to help you do that today. Transform lead into gold and be pleased with your result.

Thursday 14th

As the Moon enters your carer sector, you are emotionally drawn to review your status. Are you where you want to be? Could you add a small goal to your work prospects? You may feel anxious or rebellious and this may cause some unrest. Watch your words today.

Friday 15th

Any emotional state you are already in will be exaggerated, today. Jupiter likes to make everything bigger and he connects with the Moon now. You may feel like the luckiest person alive and overlook the small details. Mind that Jupiter does not inflate your ego too much.

Saturday 16th

It is the weekend and once more the Moon sits in your social sector. However, you may feel at a loss of what to do. Perhaps there are no invitations for you today. The urge to connect may not be satisfied today; use this time to connect with spirit instead.

Sunday 17th

A busy day in the heavens reflects your mindset today. Your mind is overloaded with fantasy thinking. Dreams and visions appear intrusive and you wish to switch off. Have some downtime but try not to use alcohol or other unhealthy crutches, as they will take you to a place which is more frenzied.

Monday 18th

At last, Mercury turns direct and you begin to get some clarity. Any health issues you may have noticed in the last few weeks should now be addressed. The plans in your head, your vision board and your search for a new focus will now become easier to access.

Tuesday 19th

The Moon opposite newly direct Mercury means that you have an emotional heart-to-heart with yourself. Forgive yourself for any time you felt in jeopardy. Do not go down the self-blame route as it is now closed. Introspection will give you valuable insights into your conditioned behaviour.

Wednesday 20th

Today you feel tired and lack motivation. Stick with it, as this will pass. A Full Moon in your dreams sector may highlight the need for you to spend time alone. It may also show you that you have too many things on the go and your mind cannot hold them all.

Thursday 21st

The Moon now sits in your own sign and you may feel rather selfish. Like a small child, you will be prone to tantrums if you do not get your own way. There might be a struggle with someone in authority who attempts to pull you out of this mood.

Friday 22nd

There might be more conflict today. You could be stamping your feet and raging at what you perceive as a personal injustice. The two ruling planets of your opposite sign are arguing, and you will see some of your darker side as your shadow is triggered. This needs to be healed now.

Saturday 23rd

The Sun enters your relationship sector, and this can go two ways for you. Either this can be a warm and healing time with a special person, or it could show you exactly where you project your shadow onto another. What you dislike about someone is actually something inside you.

Sunday 24th

Conversations around money and value will be on the agenda today. How you place value onto material things will be up for discussion. As a Taurus you will naturally love money and possessions, but not all people do. It is time to look at and review any joint investments.

Monday 25th

A fantasy or illusion you have been harbouring may now come crashing down around you. It could be that you see the real person instead of the image you have projected onto them. By the time evening comes, you will be craving for the old and familiar feeling of days past.

Tuesday 26th

You need to be around those who can nurture you. Home comforts or family favourite meals are just the things to nourish you today. You could be licking your wounds after a reality check. Mothers or female friendships are helpful and will offer a good place for you to recover.

Wednesday 27th

If you are finding it hard to express your basic need, then tune into your intuition. Listen to what it is telling you. You will need to excavate your deep, dark areas and take away your safety blanket for now. This can be an emotionally difficult day for you.

Thursday 28th

As the Moon shifts into your family sector, you should find yourself feeling tired but safe. Security means a lot to you now and being with family and loved ones can help. Your ruler, Venus, connects with Jupiter and sends you luck and love. Harmony within you can be restored now.

Friday 29th

Although you have now regained some joy, there will always be something or someone who will try and bring you down. You may be on shaky ground with a family member. Sibling rivalry is possible. The good thing is that you are able to get things off your chest now.

Saturday 30th

Mars enters your relationship sector which is likely to stir things up. Mars is associated with our energy and sex drive and is the ruler of this sign. You could be in for a steamy time with a lover or a period of rows and aggression. Watch this space.

Sunday 31st

The Moon returns to your creative sector. As this sector also deals with falling in love, perhaps you have rekindled a relationship or made apologies for upsets made during Mercury retrograde. Planetary energy is easier now and relating with others should be more straightforward. Be kind and selfless, and you will be rewarded.

NOVEMBER
. . . .

Monday 1st

Are you fighting the mists of Neptune? Sometimes you are asked to go with the flow but keep a tow line connected to land. At these times, it is difficult for you to stay in the moment. A tendency to over-drink, over-eat or self-medicate is likely now.

Tuesday 2nd

Mundane jobs need your attention. If you can get to grips with things that need doing, then you can free up some time for health or leisure activities. You might struggle with someone trying to control how you spend your time. Saturn allows you the grace to deal with this with kindness.

Wednesday 3rd

The Moon meets up with Mercury today. Filtering information that comes your way may bring about an emotional response. You may also be more inclined to go over the top with these emotions. Triggers happen for you to recognise and deal with. Look at how you habitually react and respond.

Thursday 4th

A New Moon in your opposite sign offers a chance to deal with your darker side. Issues concerning relating, sex, death and rebirth are good starting points. Aggression or sexual passion will be high today. Remember that the other person has feelings too. Be mindful and remember boundaries.

Friday 5th

Mercury now enters your relationship sector. He will assist you in having those deep conversations about the meaning of life and the universe. Venus also moves today; she will now enter your travel sector. Perhaps these two signify a travel opportunity to mysterious lands to explore with your partner.

Saturday 6th

Today has lighter energy. You may be looking back at things you have enjoyed in the past. Again, travel is the theme. You might yearn to re-visit a place where you have felt at home. Might this be a good opportunity to introduce a partner to a piece of your past?

Sunday 7th

Your mind is still wandering off to distant lands. You could satisfy this by watching documentaries, reading books, or looking at websites which showcase a land and people you have an affinity with. Be careful not to get trapped in a fanciful illusion now as this may disappoint when reality kicks back in. Keep it real.

Monday 8th

The Moon and Venus met up tonight and they now add a feminine touch to any travel plans you might have. You have some unusual ideas, and feel fired up thinking about how your senses will be touched by countries and philosophies you had not previously considered. Plan your itinerary.

Tuesday 9th

Think about how you can have a shared experience. You are very good at going it alone but now your wish is to have someone to enjoy it all with. Plan ahead, take small steps and get things in motion. You have the leadership skills to do this.

Wednesday 10th

Today is not so easy and it seems that any route you take has a dead end. You will get frustrated and run the risk of being argumentative. The Moon is making some bad connections to difficult planets. The only saving grace you have today is that you can talk about it.

Thursday 11th

Something is growing or building in your consciousness. You want to get it all out but now is not the time. This evening, Jupiter lends you some of his expansiveness and whatever is eating at you gets bigger. Hold it a little while longer.

Friday 12th

Today would be a good day to look to your tribe and ask for advice and personal experiences similar to your plans. Your ruler helps you to balance what is good and bad information. Stay in that holding space and consider all your options. Friends and social groups are invaluable now. Connect and learn.

Saturday 13th

Planetary energy lifts at first but, once more, you are lost in a sea of fantasy. Your mind is now swimming with far too much information. It is likely that you will blurt out your latest ideas and look a fool. Knowing you, you will feel hurt but will not change anything.

Sunday 14th

Social groups can be overwhelming now. You wish you had not spoken too soon. However, your friends mean well and want you to understand that. This afternoon, you welcome the chance to switch off and be alone with your thoughts and dreams. They have become too precious for you to lose.

Monday 15th

In your own little world, you consider your responsibilities and come back down to earth. You needed to do this in your own time. Even though this goes against your nature you know that, if it is not dealt with, there will be trouble down the line.

Tuesday 16th

Watch out for ego clashes today. The Sun's in your opposite sign and the Moon is in your dreams sector; your partner could win. You might have truth and justice on your side from Jupiter, but the planet of control Pluto is against you. Take it on the chin and retreat if you must.

Wednesday 17th

This morning, the Moon shifts into your sign. Unfortunately, this does not bring relief. Saturn restricts your movement, and Mars and Uranus stand off. This makes for a lot of tension. Something is going to blow. Are you the volcano in this scenario?

Thursday 18th

Your feelings are very close to the surface now. Although there are helpful connections to Neptune who can soften and dissolve arguments, there are harder connections from the Moon in your sign to the more volatile planets. Today, it is probably better to stay in bed. This war is not over yet.

Friday 19th

A Full Moon in your sign is the perfect spotlight for the recent troubles. You can clearly see now how things came to this. People will be pointing the finger; let it not be at you. Venus softens any further disruption and Pluto helps transmute it into something better.

Saturday 20th

Your finances and possessions come under scrutiny today. You may be tempted to over-spend as a way to lift up your spirits, but this is not the answer. Saturn asks you to spend responsibly and you will be rewarded in another way. Treat yourself to a good old Taurean dining experience instead.

Sunday 21st

The influence of Neptune today means that you need to keep as grounded as possible. Using addictions as ways to cover up wounds that need healing is not the answer. As Jupiter is involved here too, anything you do or feel today will get out of hand.

Monday 22nd

Come morning, your emotional body needs home comfort and nurturing. The Sun now warms up your intimacy sector and Venus and Mars make a good connection. Find someone that you love or have high regard for and share a hug or two. Offloading to a special person works wonders.

Tuesday 23rd

Although the Moon sits opposite your ruler, Venus, you still manage to have an emotionally satisfying day. Irritability and frustration become calm. This could be by family members. Mothers, in particular, have a big role to play today. Listen to older women and appreciate their wisdom.

Wednesday 24th

When being nurtured, make sure that you aren't in fact being manipulated. Make messages short and sweet. Late this afternoon, you should feel re-energised. Mercury is at the final degree of your relationship sector and asks that you make sure all is well before he goes adventuring in your deep intimacy sector.

Thursday 25th

Today, co-operation between sexes comes easy. You will want to express yourself loudly but dumb yourself down so that another can shine. How nice of you. In doing this, you are shining a stronger light and leading by example. You may reminisce with family members.

Friday 26th

Maybe you just cannot resist being the centre of attention today. You gave the spotlight to someone else and now you are snatching it back. This is likely to make you very unpopular. Jupiter is right opposite and watching as you inflate your ego in a way which displeases him.

Saturday 27th

The Moon drifts back into your creative sector. You may have a bruised ego now and wish to make amends. However, whatever comes out of your mouth now will not be good enough. Emotions and self-awareness are out of sync. Give up and try again another day.

Sunday 28th

Today is another one of those days where you just want to switch off and be alone. Try doing this in a constructive way. Do you have any paperwork or admin that needs attention? Today is perfect for editing, filing and other general admin tasks. Start the new week with a tidy mind and home space.

Monday 29th

This morning the Moon enters your health and duties sector. Get your head down and stuck into work. This will ease the tension you have built up within you. Mercury is in the heat of the Sun so your mind could be busy with whatever task you set it to today.

Tuesday 30th

Your responsibilities come first today. Venus may try to cajole you into fantasy land, but you resist. A lot of good planetary connections to Saturn help you get the job done and with time to spare. A session at the gym will finish the day off well. Treat yourself to a healthy smoothie, too.

DECEMBER

. . . .

Wednesday 1st

Your relationship sector is highlighted today. Neptune, the planet that can dissolve established structures, goes direct now. You may have some clarity in relationship concerns. Suddenly, all is not as it once was. Anything that was once solid may now begin to crumble. Let it go.

Thursday 2nd

Your sense of self is threatened today as a Scorpio Moon throws light on your shadow. You feel resistance to this, but Neptune asks that you go with the flow. What you resist will persist. Triggers are the key to your unresolved business. You will feel uncomfortable, but you will grow.

Friday 3rd

You are after something and determined that you will have it. This could be a sexy night with a lover as the Moon meets up with hot-headed Mars. Aggression can also appear now under this influence. This afternoon you feel more fired up to get out and about. Use that Mars energy to do something exhilarating.

Saturday 4th

The final New Moon of the year asks that you set intentions around wider exploration. You may have a secret impulse to explore esoteric subjects or other cultures. Planning a holiday is a great thing to do under this Moon. Mercury will help you do a little research.

Sunday 5th

Today has just the right feel for a splendid Sunday afternoon. Spending time away from home will lift your spirits. Take the first steps for any new projects you have lined up. Today will also be a good day to do those jobs that need to get done. Lighter energy brings you good fortune and a spring in your step.

Monday 6th

Due to the Moon making easy connections to difficult planets, your emotions are controlled and stable. There is an element of surprise today. You may be changing your mindset about someone you once thought was important to you. Be kind and let them go with love.

Tuesday 7th

The Moon meets up with Pluto today and you may feel a little manipulated. However, other influences suggest that you are more likely to be changing a poor situation into a better one. Your career is illuminated when the Moon shifts this afternoon. Time to consider your work prospects.

Wednesday 8th

In the workplace, there can be some conflict which may cause you to lose face. Luck will not be on your side today and you may end up eating humble pie. Those in authority demand respect and like a child you are reluctant to give it. The rebel in you is riled.

Thursday 9th

Unfairness angers you today. You will be meeting up with someone who you hope can change this. There will be a lot of conversation, but do make sure that you are getting your facts right or you will be known as a gossip or rabble-rouser. Ask trusted friends for advice.

Friday 10th

Under a Moon in your social sector, you end the weekend with your tribe. You need to be with like-minded souls who understand your principles. Social media groups can support your views but be careful that you are not doing this to stroke a bruised ego.

Saturday 11th

Something which you once believed strongly may fall apart before your eyes. Your inner child may be hurt by this. Today you are not sure what you is truth and what is not. This is a passing phase, so don't fret. By late evening, your ruler soothes you and makes you more stable.

Sunday 12th

Today you are best advised to spend time alone with your thoughts. Anger is bubbling under the surface. You need to process recent events and changes. For a Taurus, this can be difficult. A short dive into the underworld of your psyche is necessary. You may even find some pearls.

Monday 13th

Two planets change sign today. Mercury enters your travel sector and wants to research future vacations. Mars marches into your sex, death and rebirth sector and wants some hot action. He will now cull anything that is not serving you in this area. He may also bring a few secrets with him.

Tuesday 14th

Stay in your own mind for a short while longer. Something has stirred within you and this needs addressing. When the Moon moves into your own sign today, this will be on the dissecting table. You may not like what you see, but you must do something with it.

Wednesday 15th

You are likely to blow a fuse today. Take note of what triggers you again. Another face-off with an authority figure or elder of your family is possible. You mind find yourself reaching back into the past and bringing forward a skill set you have not used for some time.

Thursday 16th

Today you have a better idea of the inner work you need to do. The outer planets, Neptune and Pluto, are connecting to the Moon in your sign and helping you. You get a clearer sense of self and understand the need for change. Self-love will be your motivator now.

Friday 17th

How is your bank balance? The next two days are an opportunity to organise your finances before the holiday season kicks off. You need to catch up with messages or small chores over the weekend. Saturn is pleased that you are being sensible today. Well done.

Saturday 18th

Venus, your beautiful ruler, goes retrograde today. At these times, it is important that you review where you place value and how you bring peace and harmony. You may see a face from the past or a love affair might fall apart. Venus will be hanging around in your travel sector, causing a few upsets.

Sunday 19th

A Full Moon in your money sector advises you to look at where you may have over-spent this year, as it may be taking its toll now when you need it. A family day will be nurturing as an early seasonal get-together satisfies your emotional needs. Plan for the festivities now.

Monday 20th

Mercury and the Moon both connect to Uranus in your sign. This signifies early surprises as pleasant energy flows easily. You might have to curb what you say if one of those surprises is not to your taste. You must choose whether to speak from your head or your heart.

Tuesday 21st

It is the Winter Solstice and the longest night. This is the perfect time to hunker down with all your favourite comfort foods and entertainment. Someone may try to take control, but you can let them know there is no need. You know best how to nourish yourself.

Wednesday 22nd

Being with family brings out your inner child. You feel happy to be with those who know you best and where you can truly express yourself unfiltered. You may come across some opposition regarding breaching another's boundaries. Leave them alone and enjoy them for who they are.

Thursday 23rd

Jupiter is at the last degree of your career sector. If you have not already shut down for the holidays, check if there is anything crucial that you need to complete now. The planet of joy, who is much like Santa Claus, would like you to enjoy the season without extra worries.

Friday 24th

A busy day in the heavens means that last minute shopping or arrangements are highly likely. There is much to do and the Moon's connections to disruptive planets is not going to make it easy. Watch that temper and pull your weight today; there is too much at stake.

Saturday 25th

If there is a female who tries to take control today, let them. Venus has met Pluto in her retrograde and she will not be happy feeling powerless. As she is your ruler, you will probably feel this intensely. It may be difficult to relax, but do not do this with too much alcohol.

Sunday 26th

Beautiful connections from the Moon mean that today is far more relaxing. The hard work has been done and you can kick back and enjoy yourself. There is a balance of duties by this evening and you feel satisfied that all has gone well. Well done for doing your part.

. . . .

Monday 27th

You feel energised and buoyant today. You have had a
responsible festive season so far and Saturn is pleased with
you. Use the energy from Mars to ensure you stay focused and
visit friends and relatives you have missed. This could also be a
great day for intimate connections.

Tuesday 28th

Today is not likely to be so easy for you. The Venus retrograde
might already be causing a fuss in your outgoing travel sector.
There may be arguments or simply disagreements, as not
everyone is on the same page today. Mind what you say with
sensitive people and back down if you must.

Wednesday 29th

The Moon in your relationship sector asks that you spend
some time with a special person. As usual, this can mean that
you are triggered, but for good reason. Jupiter enters your
social sector today. Prepare for a year where your friendships
and groups get much bigger and more active.

Thursday 30th

Time spent with a partner will be deep and mysterious now.
Conversations can border on the taboo but do not offend. If
you are a night owl, you will feel a little more anxious and
possibly judged in the late hours. Do not take it too personally.

Friday 31st

There is only one way to end the year for you. Your emotions and sex drive are in sync so grab your partner and reminisce on what went well in 2021. Get those travel brochures out and expand your horizons. Set your sights on making next year a big adventure.

Taurus

....

PEOPLE WHO SHARE
YOUR SIGN

PEOPLE WHO
SHARE YOUR SIGN

. . . .

Ambitious Taureans dominate in their professional fields, and their tenacity has seen many rise to fame throughout history and in the present day. From famous singers like Adele and Ella Fitzgerald, to top models such as Gigi Hadid and renowned artists like Salvador Dalí, the beauty that Taureans bring into the world is evident. Discover the creative Taureans who share your exact birthday and see if you can spot any similarities.

21st April
Jessey Stevens (1992), James McAvoy (1979), Steve Backshall (1973), Robert Smith (1959), Iggy Pop (1947), Diana Darvey (1945), Queen Elizabeth II of the United Kingdom (1926), Charlotte Brontë (1816)

22nd April
Louis Smith (1989), Tyra Sanchez (1988), Michelle Ryan (1984), Daniel Johns (1973), Jack Nicholson (1937), Glen Campbell (1936), Immanuel Kant (1724), Queen Isabella I of Castile (1451)

23rd April
Gigi Hadid (1995), Taio Cruz (1980), Jaime King (1979), John Cena (1977), Kal Penn (1977), Michael Moore (1954), Sandra Dee (1942), Shirley Temple (1928), Dorian Leigh (1917), James Buchanan, U.S. President (1791), William Shakespeare (1564)

24th April

Casper Lee (1994), Joe Keery (1992), Kelly Clarkson (1982), Austin Nichols (1980), Cedric the Entertainer (1964), Barbra Streisand (1942), Shirley MacLaine (1934)

25th April

Joslyn Davis (1982), Alejandro Valverde (1980), Tim Duncan (1976), Renée Zellweger (1969), Hank Azaria (1964), Len Goodman (1944), Al Pacino (1940), Ella Fitzgerald (1917), Oliver Cromwell (1599)

26th April

Luke Bracey (1989), Jemima Kirke (1985), Channing Tatum (1980), Melania Trump (1970), Kevin James (1965), Giancarlo Esposito (1958), Roger Taylor (1949), Carol Burnett (1933)

27th April

Froy Gutierrez (1998), Jenna Coleman (1986), Patrick Stump (1984), Darcey Bussell (1969), Tess Daly (1969), Coretta Scott King (1927), Ulysses S. Grant, U.S. President (1822)

28th April

Melanie Martinez (1995), Jessica Alba (1981), Penélope Cruz (1974), Bridget Moynahan (1971), Diego Simeone (1970), Jay Leno (1950), Terry Pratchett (1948), Harper Lee (1926), Oskar Schindler (1908), James Monroe, U.S. President (1758)

29th April

Katherine Langford (1996), Kian Egan (1980), Uma Thurman (1970), Kolinda Grabar-Kitarović, Croatian President (1968), Michelle Pfeiffer (1958), Daniel Day-Lewis (1957), Jerry Seinfeld (1954), Willie Nelson (1933)

30th April

Travis Scott (1992), Dianna Agron (1986), Gal Gadot (1985), Kirsten Dunst (1982), Kunal Nayyar (1981), Johnny Galecki (1975), Leigh Francis (1973), Queen Juliana of the Netherlands (1909)

1st May

Caggie Dunlop (1989), Anushka Sharma (1988), Leonardo Bonucci (1987), Jamie Dornan (1982), James Murray (1976), Wes Anderson (1969), Tim McGraw (1967), Joanna Lumley (1946), Calamity Jane (1852)

2nd May

Lily Allen (1985), Ellie Kemper (1980), David Beckham (1975), Dwayne Johnson (1972), Donatella Versace (1955), Christine Baranski (1952), James Dyson (1947), Catherine the Great (1729)

3rd May

MC Pedrinho (2002), Poppy Delevingne (1986), Rebecca Hall (1982), Eric Church (1977), Christina Hendricks (1975), Rob Brydon (1965), Frankie Valli (1934), James Brown (1933)

4th May

Alex Lawther (1995), Rory McIlroy (1989), Radja Nainggolan (1988), Francesc Fàbregas (1987), Trisha Krishnan (1983), Will Arnett (1970), Keith Haring (1958), Mick Mars (1951), Audrey Hepburn (1929)

5th May

Brooke Hogan (1988), Adele (1988), Bart Baker (1986), Henry Cavill (1983), Craig David (1981), Vincent Kartheiser (1979), Karl Marx (1818)

6th May

Mateo Kovačić (1994), Naomi Scott (1993), Meek Mill (1987), Chris Paul (1985), Dani Alves (1983), George Clooney (1961), Orson Welles (1915), Sigmund Freud (1856)

7th May

Alexander Ludwig (1992), Earl Thomas (1989), Chiara Ferragni (1987), J Balvin (1985), Breckin Meyer (1974), Michael Rosen (1946), Pyotr Ilyich Tchaikovsky (1840), Johannes Brahms (1833)

8th May

Katy B (1989), Nyle DiMarco (1989), Matt Willis·(1983), Stephen Amell (1981), Matthew Davis (1978), Enrique Iglesias (1975), David Attenborough (1926), Harry S. Truman, U.S. President (1884)

9th May

Noah Centineo (1996), Audrina Patridge (1985), Rosario Dawson (1979), Ghostface Killah (1970), John Corbett (1961), Billy Joel (1949), Candice Bergen (1946), Albert Finney (1936)

10th May

Halston Sage (1993), Lindsey Shaw (1989), Aslı Enver (1984), Linda Evangelista (1965), Bono (1960), Ellen Ochoa (1958), Sid Vicious (1957), Fred Astaire (1899)

11th May

Sabrina Carpenter (1999), Lana Condor (1997), Thibaut Courtois (1992), Blac Chyna (1988), Holly Valance (1983), Cory Monteith (1982), Jonathan Jackson (1982), Salvador Dalí (1904)

12th May

Emily VanCamp (1986), Domhnall Gleeson (1983), Malin Åkerman (1978), Jason Biggs (1978), Tony Hawk (1968), Catherine Tate (1968), Emilio Estevez (1962), Florence Nightingale (1820)

13th May

Debby Ryan (1993), Romelu Lukaku (1993), Tommy Dorfman (1992), Robert Pattinson (1986), Iwan Rheon (1985), Yaya Touré (1983), Stevie Wonder (1950), Joe Louis (1914)

14th May

Martin Garrix (1996), Miranda Cosgrove (1993), Dustin Lynch (1985), Olly Murs (1984), Mark Zuckerberg (1984), Martine McCutcheon (1976), Cate Blanchett (1969), Greg Davies (1968), George Lucas (1944)

15th May

Birdy (1996), Sophie Cookson (1990), Stella Maxwell (1990), Andy Murray (1987), Alexandra Breckenridge (1982), Zara Tindall (1981), Ray Lewis (1975), Brian Eno (1948), Madeleine Albright (1937)

16th May

Thomas Brodie-Sangster (1990), Megan Fox (1986), Billy Crawford (1982), Tori Spelling (1973), David Boreanaz (1969), Janet Jackson (1966), Pierce Brosnan (1953), Danny Trejo (1944)

17th May

AJ Mitchell (2001), Charlotte Crosby (1990), Ross Butler (1990), Nikki Reed (1988), Tahj Mowry (1986), Passenger (1984), Kandi Burruss (1976), Jordan Knight (1970), Enya (1961), Bob Saget (1956), Bill Paxton (1955), Gary Paulsen (1939)

18th May

Madilyn Paige (1997), KYLE (1993), Jack Johnson (1975), Tina Fey (1970), Miriam Margolyes (1941), Pope John Paul II (1920), Perry Como (1912), Fred Perry (1909)

19th May

JoJo Siwa (2003), Marshmello (1992), Sam Smith (1992), Eleanor Tomlinson (1992), Lily Cole (1987), Kiera Cass (1981), Yo Gotti (1981), Kevin Garnett (1976), Israel Houghton (1971), Grace Jones (1948), Peter Mayhew (1944), Malcom X (1925)

20th May

Matt Terry (1993), Jon Pardi (1985), Naturi Naughton (1984), Rachel Platten (1981), Busta Rhymes (1972), Mary Pope Osborne (1949), Cher (1946), James Stewart (1908)

21st May

Tom Daley (1994), Mario Mandzukic (1986), Gotye (1980), Noel Fielding (1973), The Notorious B.I.G. (1972), Mark Crilley (1966), Mr. T (1952)